Miriam Windham
Spring 2000

P9-DID-919

Quest

Listening and Speaking in the Academic World,
Book 2

Laurie Blass

McGraw Hill

Boston   Burr Ridge, IL   Dubuque, IA   Madison, WI
New York   San Francisco   St. Louis
Bangkok   Bogotá   Caracas   Lisbon   London
Madrid   Mexico City   Milan   New Delhi   Seoul
Singapore   Sydney   Taipei   Toronto

McGraw-Hill Higher Education

A Division of The **McGraw-Hill** *Companies*

QUEST: LISTENING AND SPEAKING IN THE ACADEMIC WORLD, BOOK 2

This book is printed on acid-free paper.

1 2 3 4 5 6 7 8 9 0 QPF/QPF 0 9 8 7 6 5 4 3 2 1 0

ISBN 0–07–006252–8

Vice president and editorial director: *Thalia Dorwick*
Publisher: *Tim Stookesberry*
Developmental editor: *Aurora Martinez Ramos*
Marketing manager: *Pam Tiberia*
Project manager: *Joyce M. Berendes*
Production supervisor: *Sandy Ludovissy*
Designer: *Michael Warrell*
Senior photo research coordinator: *Carrie K. Burger*
Supplement coordinator: *Sandra M. Schnee*
Compositor: *David Corona Design*
Typeface: *10/12 Times Roman*
Printer: *Quebecor Printing Book Group/Fairfield, PA*

Cover designer: *Victory Productions*
Cover image: *Lonnie Sue Johnson*
Photo research: *Toni Michaels*

INTERNATIONAL EDITION ISBN 0–07–116388–3

www.mhhe.com

contents

121533

preface

Quest: The Series

The *Quest* series addresses the need to prepare students for the demands of college-level academic coursework. *Quest* differs from other content-based ESOL series in that it incorporates material typically covered in general education courses, and contains a variety of academic areas including biology, business, history, psychology, art history, anthropology, literature, and economics.

Quest has been designed to parallel and accelerate the process that native speakers of English go through when they study core required subjects in high school. By previewing typical college course material, *Quest* helps students get "up to speed" in terms of both academic content and language skills.

In addition, *Quest* prepares students for the daunting amount and level of reading, writing, listening, and speaking required for college success. The three *Reading and Writing* books combine high-interest material from newspapers and magazines with traditional academic source materials such as textbooks. Reading passages increase in length and difficulty across the three levels. The *Listening and Speaking* books in the *Quest* series contain listening strategies and practice activities based on recorded conversations among college students, authentic "person-on-the-street" interviews, radio programs, and college lectures. Similar to the *Reading and Writing* books, the three *Listening and Speaking* books increase in difficulty within each level and between levels.

The *Quest Listening and Speaking* books have been coordinated with the *Reading and Writing* books so that the two, used in conjunction, provide students with complementary, overlapping, yet distinct information—much as happens in a typical college class, in which students attend a lecture on a given topic and then complete textbook reading assignments on a related topic.

Quest: Listening and Speaking in the Academic World, Book 2

Quest: Listening and Speaking in the Academic World, Book 2 contains four distinct units, each focusing on a different area of college study—business, art, psychology, and health. Each content unit contains two chapters. The business unit is comprised of chapters on doing business internationally and international economy. The art unit includes chapters on themes and purposes and ancient Greek art. The chapters in the psychology unit concentrate on states of consciousness and abnormal psychology, and the final unit, health, focuses on medicine and drugs and the secrets of good health.

Unique to this series is the inclusion of three different *types* of listening passages in each chapter:

- Everyday English—an informal conversation among college students (or in some chapters, person-on-the-street interviews)—on both audiotape and videotape;

- Broadcast English—an authentic radio segment from such sources as National Public Radio and Public Radio International; and

- Academic English—a short college lecture

Unique Chapter Structure

Each chapter of *Quest: Listening and Speaking in the Academic World, Book 2* contains five parts that blend listening, speaking, and academic skills within the content of a particular area of study. In Part One, pictures, charts, and/or a short reading provide the basis for discussion and response writing and prepare students for the listening passages that follow. In Part Two, Everyday English, students listen to and use informal, conversational English related to the chapter theme. Part Three, The Mechanics of Listening and Speaking, focuses on language functions, pronunciation, and intonation; it culminates in an activity requiring students to make use of all three of these areas. In Part Four, Broadcast English, students learn to understand and discuss an authentic radio passage which, in turn, helps to prepare them for the lecture that follows. Part Five, Academic English, presents an audiotaped lecture on the chapter theme and guides students toward proficient note-taking skills; the final activity in the chapter, Step Beyond, involves students in discussion, original research, and presentation of their own findings.

Supplements*

The Instructor's Manual to accompany *Quest: Listening and Speaking in the Academic World, Books 1-3* provides instructors with a general outline of the series, as well as detailed teaching suggestions and important information regarding levels and placement, classroom management, and chapter organization. For each of the three books, there is a separate section with answer keys, oral practice, and unit tests. In addition, there is an audio/video component to accompany each of the three *Quest: Listening and Speaking* books.

Acknowledgments

Many, many thanks go to those who have made and are making this series possible: Marguerite Ann Snow, who provided the initial inspiration for this entire series; publisher for ESOL, Tim Stookesberry, who first said *yes;* vice president and editorial director Thalia Dorwick, who made it happen; editor Aurora Martinez Ramos, who gave encouragement and support and helped shape the manuscript; marketing manager Pam Tiberia, who guides the books into classrooms; Joe Higgins of National Public Radio, who went above-and-beyond to help us find one especially wonderful but elusive tape; the many students who have tried materials and let us know what worked and what didn't; the good people at Mannic Productions and Paul Ruben Productions, Inc.; the entire production team in Dubuque; and the following reviewers, whose opinions and suggestions were invaluable: Marietta Urban, Karen Davy, and Mark Litwicki.

---

*The supplements listed here accompany *Quest: Listening and Speaking in the Academic World, Books 1-3*. Please contact your local McGraw-Hill representative for details concerning policies, prices, and availability as some restrictions may apply.

visual tour Highlights of this Book

Chapter Four Ancient Greek Art   111

C. Reading about Ancient Greek Civilization and Art. Read the following passage about
Greek civilization and art. As you read, try to answer this question:

• Why are Greek vases so important?

Greek Civilization and Art

No doubt a major reason that we respect the ancient Greeks is that they
excelled in many different fields. Their political ideals serve as a model
for contemporary democracy. Their poetry and drama and philosophy
survive as living classics, familiar to every serious scholar. Their architecture
5 and sculpture have influenced most later periods in the history of Western art.
    We assume that the Greeks' genius shone equally in painting,
very little about this because most painted works have been los
know even less, except that a large number of painted clay vases w
from about the 8th century B.C. These pots were made from **terra**
10 clay), an extremely strong material; it can break, but it won't disi
so the pieces can be reassembled. For this reason a large quantity
has survived to our day.

112   Unit 2 Art

D. Comprehension Check. Group Discuss the answers to these questions.

1. Why are Greek vases so important?
2. What were Greek vases made from? Why did they last so long?
3. Describe the painting style of the *Dipylon Vase*.
4. What does the *Dipylon Vase* tell us about ancient Greek civilization?
5. How were the ancient Greeks different from the ancient Egyptians?

E. Response Writing. Choose *one* of these topics. Write about it for ten minutes. Don't worry
about grammar and don't use a dictionary. Just put as many ideas as you can on paper.

• Describe what you know or remember about ancient Greek civilization, Greek myths and
  legends, or ancient Greek art.
• Write about what you would like to know about ancient Greek civilization, Greek myths and
  legends, or ancient Greek art.
• Compare the *Dipylon Vase* to another work of art, from any time or civilization.
• Have you been to Greece? If so, describe your experience.

Part One: Focus on Activating Prior Knowledge with Practice Opportunities in all Language Skills

Part One of each chapter contains a variety of high-interest activities that gradually introduce students to the chapter topic. Prior to reading, students are given the opportunity to think ahead and discuss what they already know about ancient Greece. After reading a brief passage about Greek civilization and art, students answer discussion questions and complete a response writing activity in which they share their reactions to the chapter topic or their knowledge of the subject matter. (pages 111 and 112)

Part Two Everyday English: Greek Pottery

Before Listening

A. Thinking Ahead. Group You are
going to listen to Tanya and a teaching
assistant, Doug, talk about one type of
Greek art: pottery. Before you listen, look
at this photo of Greek pottery and discuss
the images on it in your groups.
    As you did in Chapter Three, de-
scribe your impressions. Interpret what
you see. Remember to trust your instincts:
You know more than you think you know.
Who might the people be? Where do you
think the idea for the picture came from?

Interior of a *kylix*, a drinking cup. Around 490–480 B.C.

Emphasis on Listening Preparation

All listening passages are preceded by prelistening activities such as thinking ahead, discussion, prediction, and vocabulary preparation. In this example, students observe a photo of a Greek drinking cup dated around 490–480 B.C. *Eos and Memnon,* and interpret the image in the cup. In order to prepare them for the listening passage found later in this part of the chapter, students are also encouraged to describe their impressions about the photo. (page 112)

Listening

A. Listening for the Main Idea. Video/Audio   Now listen to the conversation. As you liste[n]
to answer this question:

• Why is Greek pottery so important in the study of ancient Greek culture?

---

116   Unit 2   Art

After Listening

A. Information Gap. Pair Work with a partner. One of you works on page 117. The other works
on page 275. Don't look at your partner's page. You both will ask and answer questions and complete
a chart.

Student A

It's a good idea to review Greek myths and legends when you study ancient Greek art. This is because
ancient Greek art often **depicts** (shows) subjects from myths and legends. An important part of
Greek mythology is the gods and goddesses. People who study art need to know their Greek and
Roman names and the characteristics or activities that they represent. How much do you already
know about them? (Refer to the vocabulary chart for help with difficult words.)

Ask your partner for the missing information and write the answers on your chart. Take turns
asking and answering questions. Ask questions such as the following:

A: What is Aphrodite the goddess of?
B: Love and beauty.

Icons Provide Clear Instruction

All speaking activities in the book are labeled for pair, group, or class practice. Listening activities are accompanied by icons that tell
whether the materials are available in audio or video formats (or both). (pages 114 and 116)

C. Listening for Inferences. Video/Audio   Now listen again. This time you are going to hear the
first part of the conversation. Listen for the answer to this question.

• Why do you think Doug interrupts his phone call?

_____

_____

_____

D. Guessing Meaning from Context: Academic Life. Video/Audio   Tanya and Doug use some
terms that describe academic life. Listen to parts of their conversation. Guess the meanings of these
terms in context. Write your guesses in the blanks.

1. office hours = _____

2. reading list = _____

Conversational Listening Practice Featured in Part Two

In **Part Two,** students are given a chance to hear
authentic conversational language on topics relevant
to their interests and everyday concerns. In addition,
these listening passages are available in both audio
and video formats providing students with the
opportunity to study the types of nonverbal cues
that accompany oral messages. (page 115)

Part Three: Focus on the Mechanics of Listening and Speaking

Part Three is devoted to providing students with
listening and speaking skills that focus on intonation,
stress, pronunciation, and various language functions.
Here, students learn about the language function of
requesting an explanation, and the intonation tip focuses
on understanding interjections typically found in
informal conversation. (pages 118 and 119)

Language Function

Requesting an Explanation Audio

Sometimes in a conversation you have difficulty understanding more than just a word or express[ion]
you don't understand an idea or a suggestion. When this happens, you ask for an explanation. H[ere]
are some ways to ask for an explanation:

Examples: A: What you need are very good photos of the pottery.

B: Why?   **Less Formal**

Well, what's the reason for that?

Can you tell me why?

Excuse me,* but why is that?

Excuse me, but why do you say that?

Excuse me, but would you mind explaining that?   **More Formal**

*Note: Adding "excuse me" makes the request more polite.

Intonation

Understanding Interjections Audio

Several interjections in English are common in informal conversation. They are very informal. Listen
to this one from the conversation:

Doug: Well, what can I do for you?

Tanya: Uh, you know that paper that's due on Friday?

Here are some more examples.

Interjections	Meanings
• Uh-huh.*	Yes. OR:
	You're welcome.
• Uh-uh.*	No.
• Huh?	What? (Excuse me?)
• Uh . . . OR:	I'm thinking. OR:
Um . . .	I'm not sure what to say.
• Uh-oh!	I made a mistake. OR:
	There's a problem.

*Note: Uh-HUH (meaning "yes") is stressed on the second syllable. UH-uh (meaning "no") is stressed on the first
syllable. This is an easy way to tell them apart.

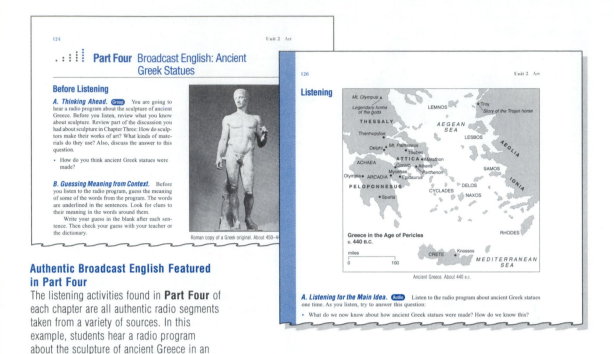

Authentic Broadcast English Featured in Part Four

The listening activities found in **Part Four** of each chapter are all authentic radio segments taken from a variety of sources. In this example, students hear a radio program about the sculpture of ancient Greece in an interview with Jacki Lyden on National Public Radio. The pages in this section where the listening activities appear include a shaded bar to indicate that the activities can be done in the language laboratory, at home, or in the classroom. (pages 124 and 126)

Abundance of Practice Material

All listening sections in *Quest* are accompanied by a variety of activities that provide students with practice opportunities to complete before, during, and after hearing the passage. In these examples, students gain practice in the skills of listening for details. (pages 126 and 127)

Strategy Boxes Sharpen Students' Skills

Listening Strategy and Speaking Strategy boxes occur frequently throughout each chapter, providing students with practical skills that they can use immediately as they work on the different listening passages. These strategy boxes are always followed by practice activities that allow students to master the strategy at hand. (pages 128 and 129)

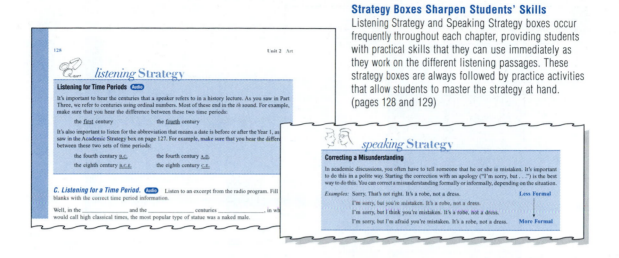

128   Unit 2 Art

listening Strategy

Listening for Time Periods Audio

It's important to hear the centuries that a speaker refers to in a history lecture. As you saw in Part Three, we refer to centuries using ordinal numbers. Most of these end in the *th* sound. For example, make sure that you hear the difference between these two time periods:

the first century   the fourth century

It's also important to listen for the abbreviation that means a date is before or after the Year 1, as saw in the Academic Strategy box on page 127. For example, make sure that you hear the differe between these two sets of time periods:

the fourth century B.C.   the fourth century A.D.

the eighth century B.C.E.   the eighth century C.E.

C. Listening for a Time Period. Audio   Listen to an excerpt from the radio program. Fill blanks with the correct time period information.

Well, in the _____ and the _____ centuries _____, in wh would call high classical times, the most popular type of statue was a naked male.

speaking Strategy

Correcting a Misunderstanding

In academic discussions, you often have to tell someone that he or she is mistaken. It's important to do this in a polite way. Starting the correction with an apology ("I'm sorry, but . . .") is the best way to do this. You can correct a misunderstanding formally or informally, depending on the situation.

Examples: Sorry. That's not right. It's a robe, not a dress.   **Less Formal**

I'm sorry, but you're mistaken. It's a robe, not a dress.

I'm sorry, but I think you're mistaken. It's a robe, not a dress.

I'm sorry, but I'm afraid you're mistaken. It's a robe, not a dress.   **More Formal**

Listening Focus in Part Five: Authentic Academic Lectures

The listening passages in each chapter of *Quest* increase in length and complexity, and culminate with an academic lecture in **Part Five.** These lectures were written by content experts in each subject area and adapted to meet the special needs of English language students. A variety of activities accompany each lecture. In this example, students learn how to listen for main ideas and for meaning in context. The lecture in this chapter, *Ancient Greek Art,* was written by Dr. Jacqueline A. Frank. (page 132)

132   Unit 2 Art

Listening

A. Listening for the Main Idea. Audio   Listen to the lecture one time. Don't take notes. Don't worry about understanding everything. Just listen for the main idea. As you listen, try to answer this question:

• What three kinds of Greek art does the speaker discuss in this lecture?

B. Listening for Meaning in Context. Audio   Listen to parts of the lecture. You will hear the speaker give definitions of some terms. Listen for the meanings of the terms. Write the definitions that you hear using your own words in the blanks.

1. kouros = _____

Academic Strategy Boxes

Found in each chapter, these strategy boxes prepare students to be active participants in the academic environment. In this example, students are given instruction in how to interpret time periods. (page 141)

academic Strategy

Interpreting Time Periods Audio

Sometimes a speaker will refer to a time period precisely, for example, "between 480 and 320 B.C.E." Sometimes, however, a speaker may refer to a time period more generally, for example, "the third century." It's a good idea to be able to go back and forth from the specific to the general time periods when you are listening to a history lecture.

Practice.   Work with a partner. Use the timeline on page 140. Use the periods in the timeline and make up your own. Say a specific time period to your partner. Your partner will then write the corresponding century into the "Centuries" column. Then switch roles.

Examples: A: [Says] 700 to 600 B.C.E.

B: [Writes] 7ᵗʰ century.

B: [Says] 550 to 600 B.C.E.

A: [Writes] 6ᵗʰ century.

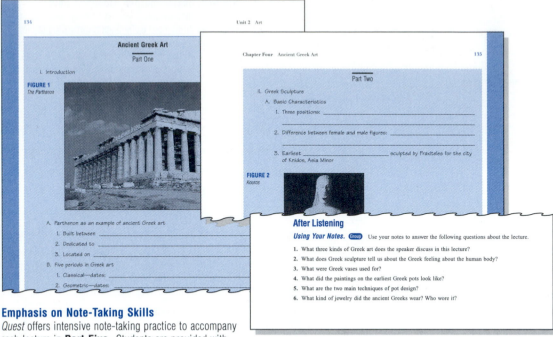

Emphasis on Note-Taking Skills

Quest offers intensive note-taking practice to accompany each lecture in **Part Five.** Students are provided with structured outlines to assist them in taking accurate notes. Moreover, well-organized postlistening activities teach students how to use and refer to their notes in order to answer both general and specific questions about the lecture. (pages 134, 135, and 141)

Step Beyond: Chapter-Culminating Speaking Activities

Each chapter ends with a *Step Beyond* speaking activity. The content of this activity takes the form of a presentation, a debate, a survey, or an interview. It is based on the chapter's theme and incorporates the listening and speaking skills that students have practiced in previous sections. In this example, students first do research on a topic of their choice and then give a presentation. (pages 142 and 143)

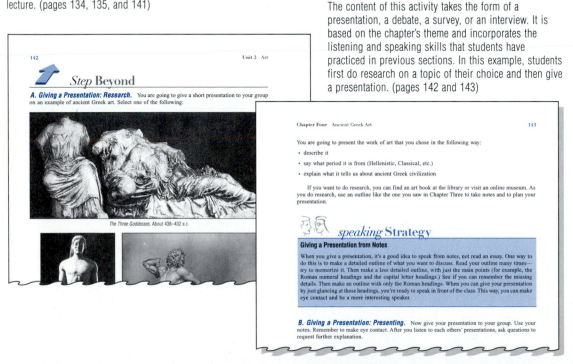

summary of Listening and Speaking Skills

Chapter	Listening/Speaking Strategies	Mechanics/Academic Strategies
1	• listening for numerical information • listening for an example • taking lecture notes • organizing your notes • listening for differences • listening for the meaning of new words and expressions • taking turns	• asking for confirmation • using tag questions to ask for confirmation • tag question intonation • confirming understanding • reduced forms in verbs followed by *to* • finding a culture informant • asking questions before you listen
2	• understanding the passive voice • guessing meaning from context: *that is* • using a quotation to illustrate an idea • listening for causes and effects • predicting • compromising • making eye contact	• asking for permission • giving and refusing permission • answering "Do/Would you mind. . . ? • intonation: *yes/no* questions • reduced forms in questions with *-d + you* • using abbreviations in note-taking
3	• using similes to guess meaning • listening for impressions or opinions • viewing images as you listen • using examples to understand new terms • forming and expressing an opinion • trusting your instincts	• asking for clarification: general • asking for clarification: specific • offering clarification • intonation: *wh-* questions • /i/ vs. /ɪ/ • using technical terms
4	• listening for time periods • using a timeline to take notes • using phonetic symbols • correcting a misunderstanding • giving a presentation from notes	• requesting an explanation • intonation: understanding interjections • the *th* sound • understanding time abbreviations • interpreting time periods

(Continued)

Chapter	Listening/Speaking Strategies	Mechanics/Academic Strategies
5	• understanding scientific terms • understanding analogies • listening for topic change signals • asking questions and keeping the audience in mind	• avoiding answering questions • verbs ending in *-ed* • *can* vs. *can't* • <u>understanding literal and figurative language</u> • <u>separating fact from theory</u>
6	• using Greek and Latin roots to guess meaning • listening to lecture introductions • using a chart to take notes • asking questions after a presentation	• asking for information over the phone • asking someone to hold on • /ɛ/ vs. /æ/ • <u>paraphrasing</u>
7	• understanding sarcasm • listening for experts' qualifications • number shortcuts • listening for comparisons • the "grammar" of smoking	• agreeing • disagreeing • expressing degrees of agreement/disagreement • expressing an opinion • reduced forms: *a* and *of* • <u>understanding Latin terms</u>
8	• guessing the meaning of proverbs from context • using context to distinguish sounds • guessing meaning from synonyms and paraphrases • making comparisons	• giving advice • degrees of giving advice • /θ/ vs. /t/ • <u>reading questions before listening</u>

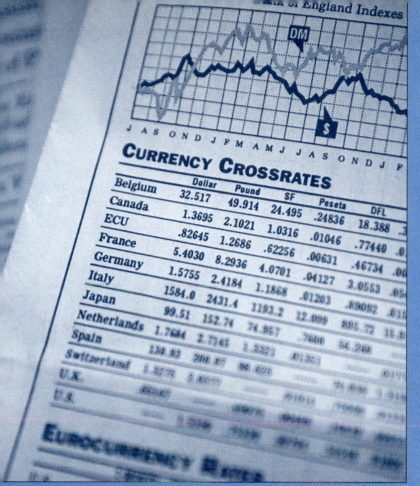

CURRENCY CROSSRATES

	Dollar	Pound	SF	Peseta	DFL
Belgium	32.517	49.914	24.495	.24836	18.388
Canada	1.3695	2.1021	1.0316	.01046	.77440
ECU	.82645	1.2686	.62256	.00631	.46734
France	5.4030	8.2936	4.0701	.04127	3.0553
Germany	1.5755	2.4184	1.1868	.01203	.89092
Italy	1584.0	2431.4	1193.2	12.099	895.72
Japan	99.51	152.74	74.957	.7600	56.298
Netherlands	1.7664	2.7145	1.3321	.01321	
Spain	130.92	206.87	98.420		
Switzerland	1.3278	2.0377		71.956	
U.K.	.65162		.01912	.7200	
U.S.					

EUROCURRENCY RATES

unit
1

Global Business

chapter One

Doing Business Internationally

In this chapter, you'll listen to information about global business and discuss the importance of recognizing cultural differences in doing business internationally.

Part One Introduction: The Ways of the World

Greeting

Tipping

Business
entertaining

Showing up
for appointments

Giving gifts

Pair   You are going to read some advice on business **etiquette** (manners) in New Zealand. The author wrote this advice for Americans who do business overseas.

Before you read, discuss with your partner whether you think New Zealanders are likely to be the same as or different from people in your culture in the situations included in the chart. Put a check (✓) next to your answers.

Same?	Different?	Situations
		Tipping (for example, a taxi driver or at a restaurant)
		Greeting business people whom you don't know well
		Being on time for a business appointment
		Places where people entertain business guests (e.g., at home, in a restaurant)
		Appropriate gifts for a business person to bring to someone's home
		Appropriate conversation topics

B. Reading.   Read the following information about etiquette in New Zealand. As you read, try to answer this question:

• Why do business travelers need this kind of information?

Etiquette in New Zealand

General Advice

• Tipping is not common, and people often refuse to take tips.

• Be prepared to be formal until others have created a more relaxed atmosphere.

Greetings

5 • Shake hands when you meet or leave someone. Wait for women to give you their hand first.

Appointments/Punctuality

• Make appointments in advance and try to arrive a bit early.

Hospitality/Gift Giving

10 • Visitors usually invite customers to lunch at a hotel or restaurant. Otherwise, business meetings will be at the host's office.

• If you are invited to a New Zealander's home for a meal, you can take a modest gift of
15 chocolates or wine, although it is not necessary.

Conversation

• New Zealanders like to talk about national and international politics, the weather, and sports. They appreciate visitors who understand their culture.

20 • Don't talk about racial issues.

• Do not include New Zealand as part of Australia or "AustralAsia and the South Pacific."

Source: Roger E. Axtell, adapted and excerpted from *Do's and Taboos Around the World, Third Edition.* Copyright © 1993 by The Parker Pen Company. Reprinted with the permission of the publisher, John Wiley & Sons, Inc.

C. Discussion. `Group`   Discuss the answers to these questions.

1. Why do you think that business people need advice on behavior in different countries?

2. Do you think advice like this is useful? Or do you think it can cause more problems? Explain your answer.

3. Have you ever had a misunderstanding because of behavior differences in two cultures? If so, describe what happened.

4. Have you ever worked in a foreign country or with people from a different culture? If so, did you have any problems? What were they?

5. Have you ever done any **personal business** in a foreign country (for example, at a bank or a post office, or buying things at a store or market)? If so, did you have any problems? What were they?

D. Response Writing.   In this book, you are going to keep a journal. In your journal, you are going to do response writing activities. In response writing, you write quickly about what you are thinking or feeling. Grammar and form are not very important in response writing. Your ideas and thoughts are important. You will have a time limit of ten minutes for your response writing in this book. You can buy a special notebook for your journal, or you can write your ideas on separate pieces of paper and keep them in a binder or folder.

Choose *one* of these topics. Write about it for ten minutes. Don't worry about grammar and don't use a dictionary. Just put as many ideas as you can on paper.

- Compare how a person from your culture might act in certain business situations with someone from New Zealand. If there are no differences, discuss similarities. Discuss one or more of the areas from the reading: tipping, greetings, appointments/punctuality, hospitality/gift giving, and appropriate conversation topics.

- Have you ever had a misunderstanding because of behavior differences in two cultures? If so, describe it.

- Have you ever experienced working with people from a different culture? What kind of conversation topics did you discuss?

. . : : : : **Part Two** Everyday English: Doing
                                   Business Overseas

Before Listening

A. Thinking Ahead. Group   You are going to listen to Victor, Tanya, and Jennifer talk about **negotiation** (discussing something in order to come to an agreement). Before you listen, discuss negotiation in your groups.

1. Often people negotiate things that have to do with money. What are some other things that people can negotiate?

2. Have you ever had to negotiate something? What was it?

3. How do you feel about negotiating? Is it easy for you? Difficult?

4. If you are good at negotiating, tell your group members some of the strategies that you use when you negotiate.

5. Have you ever had to negotiate something in a foreign country or in a foreign language? What difficulties can people have in these situations?

B. Vocabulary Preparation.   In the conversation, the students use some words and expressions that may be new to you. First, read each sentence and guess the meaning of the underlined words. Then choose their meaning from the definitions in the box. Write the letter in the blanks.

Sentences

_____ **1.** Did you know that you can <u>bargain</u> when you buy a house in the United States?

_____ **2.** I found a cheap lamp for the living room at a <u>flea market</u> last Saturday.

_____ **3.** Jennifer's a good <u>poker</u> player—she won a lot of money in last night's game.

_____ **4.** When I go on vacation, I often bring home a lot of souvenirs and <u>trinkets</u> for my friends.

_____ **5.** Some people say that the <u>key</u> to success is not giving up.

_____ **6.** The <u>asking price</u> for our house was too high, so we negotiated a lower one.

_____ **7.** He has a funny <u>ritual</u> every time he negotiates a new contract: He puts a new penny in his pocket before he goes to the meeting.

Definitions

a. the first price the seller gives

b. negotiate

c. inexpensive items

d. the most important thing

e. a market where people sell used items

f. a symbolic activity that people do over and over again, usually on special occasions

g. a card game that people play to win money

C. Guessing Meaning from Context: Idioms.

The students use some idioms in their conversation. Before you listen, guess the meaning of some words from the conversation. The words are underlined in the sentences. Look for clues to their meaning in the words around them.

Write your guess in the blank after each sentence. Then check your guess with your teacher or the dictionary.

1. Brandon wanted to see a science fiction movie and I wanted to see a romantic comedy. We kept underline going back and forth until we finally decided to see both.

   Guess: _____

2. It's late and I'm tired—I'm going to <u>turn in</u>. See you in the morning!

   Guess: _____

3. I don't like this old chair—I'm going to <u>get rid of</u> it at the flea market next Saturday.

   Guess: _____

4. Every time Evan and I try to make a date, we <u>go through</u> the same thing: He's not free at lunchtime, and I'm not free in the evenings.

   Guess: _____

Listening

A. Listening for the Main Idea. `Video/Audio` Listen to the conversation. As you listen, try to answer this question:

- What do you have to know in order to bargain in a foreign country?

B. Listening for Examples. `Video/Audio` Now listen again. This time you are going to hear only part of the conversation. Listen to Tanya and Victor's examples of the difficulties in doing personal business in a foreign country. As you listen, take notes in the chart.

	What Country Did S/he Visit?	Where Did the Problem Take Place?	What Was the Difficulty?
Tanya		bank	
Victor			

C. Listening for Details. `Video/Audio` Listen again to part of the conversation. Listen for information that answers these questions.

1. What *can* you bargain for in the United States?

_____

_____

2. What *can't* you bargain for in the United States?

_____

_____

D. Listening to an Anecdote. `Video/Audio` Tanya tells an **anecdote** (a short story) to show one way that people bargain in the United States. Listen to her anecdote and answer this question.

- Why did Tanya's dad probably get the car for the price that he wanted?

_____

_____

After Listening

A. Taking a Survey. Group Interview three people who have been to a foreign country. Ask about their experiences with doing business in their own country and in a foreign country. Write their answers in the chart.

Example: A: What have you bargained for in your country?

B: Once I bargained for a car.

Your Name	Interview 1	Interview 2	Interview 3
PART 1 Doing Business in Your Country			
1. What have you bargained for in your own country?			
2. Were you successful? If so, what was your strategy? If not, what problems did you have?			
PART 2 Doing Business in a Foreign Country			
3. What have you bargained for in a foreign country? In which country?			
4. Were you successful? If so, what was your strategy? If not, what problems did you have?			
5. Have you ever gone to a bank in a foreign country?	☐ Yes ☐ No	☐ Yes ☐ No	☐ Yes ☐ No
6. Was it the same as going to a bank in your own country?	☐ Same ☐ Different	☐ Same ☐ Different	☐ Same ☐ Different

(Continued)

7. If it was different, give an example.			
8. Have you ever had a job in a foreign country?	☐ Yes ☐ No	☐ Yes ☐ No	☐ Yes ☐ No
9. Was it the same as or different from working in your own country?	☐ Same ☐ Different	☐ Same ☐ Different	☐ Same ☐ Different
10. If it was different, give an example.			
PART 3			
Write one question of your own. _____ _____ _____ _____			

B. Discussing Survey Results. **Group**   Form small groups. Discuss the results of your survey. Try to answer these questions:

1. Do most people that you interviewed have experience bargaining? Bargaining in a foreign country?

2. Do most people feel successful at bargaining?

3. What kind of problems do people have bargaining in their own country?

4. What kinds of problems do people have bargaining in a foreign country?

5. What differences, if any, have people noticed in banking in different countries?

6. What differences, if any, have people noticed in working in a foreign country?

. .: : ¦ ¦ **Part Three** The Mechanics of Listening and Speaking

Language Function

Asking for Confirmation **Audio**

Sometimes you *think* you are right about something that a person is saying. However, you want that person to *tell* you that you are right. This is asking for confirmation. Here are some ways to ask for confirmation:

A: What I had trouble with was negotiating for stuff at the market.

B: Oh, yeah, you're not supposed to pay the asking price, <u>right</u>?

    Oh, yeah, you're not supposed to pay the asking price. <u>Isn't that right</u>?

    Oh, yeah, you're not supposed to pay the asking price. <u>Isn't that true</u>?

Notice the structure of these sentences:

                 statement of what you think is right + a question

A. Practice. **(Audio)**   Listen to Student A's information. Then ask for confirmation about it. Repeat the confirmation statements and add *right?, Isn't that right?,* or *Isn't that true?*

1. B: Oh, yeah, you're majoring in business _____?

2. B: Oh, yeah, you speak Japanese _____?

3. B: Oh, yeah, they don't line up _____?

4. B: Oh, yeah, it's impolite to discuss politics in some cultures _____?

5. B: Oh, yeah, Americans like to make small talk _____?

Language Function

Using Tag Questions to Ask for Confirmation **(Audio)**

Another way to ask for confirmation is to use a tag question. Here are some examples:

- Oh, yeah, you're not supposed to pay the asking price, <u>are you</u>?
- Oh, yeah, you're supposed to pay less than the asking price, <u>aren't you</u>?

Notice the structure of tag questions:

negative statement + affirmative tag

affirmative statement + negative tag

Also, notice that the tag matches the subject and the verb form in the statement. Here are some examples:

- <u>You speak</u> Spanish, <u>don't you</u>?
- <u>It's</u> hard to bargain in a foreign language, <u>isn't it</u>?
- <u>He doesn't</u> like it here, <u>does he</u>?
- <u>She hasn't</u> found a job yet, <u>has she</u>?
- <u>We've been</u> working hard, <u>haven't we</u>?
- <u>They're</u> working overseas, <u>aren't they</u>?
- <u>They'll</u> graduate in June, <u>won't they</u>?

Note: In tag questions with "I," the verb in the tag is plural. Here is an example:

I'm right, <u>aren't I</u>?

B. Practice.   Write the correct tag to complete each question.

1. Tanya's majoring in business, __isn't she_____?

2. Jennifer doesn't speak Spanish, _____?

3. You like working overseas, _____?

4. The professor doesn't speak very clearly, _____?

5. You've been to France, _____?

6. Victor hasn't seen the ruins yet, _____?

Intonation

Tag Question Intonation for Asking for Confirmation (Audio)

If you really need information (and you aren't sure about the answer), your voice goes up on a tag question. In other words, it's a real question. Here is an example:

You're not supposed to pay the asking price, <u>are you</u>?

However, if you know the answer, or *if you are asking for confirmation* of something that you *think* is right, your voice goes down. Here is an example:

You're not supposed to pay the asking price, <u>are you</u>?

C. Practice. (Audio)   Listen to the sentences from Exercise B. Are they "real" questions? (Does the speaker really need information?) Check (✓) *yes* or *no*. When you finish, listen again. Repeat each sentence after the speaker.

	Yes	**No**
1.	_____	_____
2.	_____	_____
3.	_____	_____
4.	_____	_____
5.	_____	_____
6.	_____	_____

D. Practice.   Complete the following confirmation questions. Use tag questions. Practice both rising and falling intonation. If the cue says DK (You don't know), use rising intonation. If it says K (You know), use falling intonation.

K   **1.** He doesn't like it here, _does he_____ ?

K   **2.** You speak Spanish, _____ ?

DK   **3.** They're working overseas, _____ ?

DK   **4.** She hasn't found a job yet, _____ ?

K   **5.** He's been working hard, _____ ?

K   **6.** You're majoring in business, _____ ?

DK   **7.** You speak Japanese, _____ ?

DK   **8.** Americans like to make small talk, _____ ?

DK   **9.** Tanya's majoring in business, _____ ?

K   **10.** Jennifer doesn't speak Spanish, _____ ?

K   **11.** You like working overseas, _____ ?

DK   **12.** You've been to France, _____ ?

K   **13.** Victor hasn't seen the ruins yet, _____ ?

Language Function

Confirming Understanding Audio

Here are some ways to confirm understanding—in other words, tell the person that you agree, or that he or she is right:

A: What I had trouble with was negotiating for stuff at the market.

B: Oh, yeah, you're not supposed to pay the asking price, right?

A: <u>Right</u>.

B: Oh, yeah, you're not supposed to pay the asking price. Isn't that right?

A: <u>That's right</u>.

B: Oh, yeah, you're not supposed to pay the asking price. Isn't that true?

A: <u>Yeah, that's true</u>.

Notice that the answer matches the form of the question at the end:

Questions		Answers
Right?	→	Right.
Isn't that right?	→	Yeah, that's right.
Isn't that true?	→	Yeah, that's true.

There is an exception. Notice what happens to the answer with a tag question:

B: Oh, yeah, you're not supposed to pay the asking price, are you?

A: <u>No, you're not</u>. (OR: <u>No, you aren't</u>.)

In this situation, you say "no" because you are agreeing with the statement—a negative statement.

E. Practice. **Audio**   Listen to Student A ask you for confirmation. Respond to the question. Tell the truth. Pay attention to tag questions.

Examples: A: You speak English, right?

You: Right. (Because you *do* speak it.)

A: You like Mexican food, don't you?

You: Yes, I do. (Because you *do* like it.)

A: You like Mexican food, don't you?

You: No, I don't. (Because you *don't* like it.)

1. You: _____ .

2. You: _____ .

3. You: _____ .

4. You: _____ .

5. You: _____ .

6. You: _____ .

Pronunciation

Reduced Forms in Verbs Followed by *to* (Audio)

When people speak quickly, some words become reduced, or short. Here are some examples of reductions in verbs followed by *to:*

Long Form

You're not <u>supposed to</u> pay the asking price.

They were probably <u>going to</u> sell it anyway.

Do you <u>want to</u> work overseas?

You <u>have to</u> know the rules of the culture.

Short Form

You're not <u>supposta</u> pay the asking price.

They were probably <u>gonna</u> sell it anyway.

Do you <u>wanna</u> work overseas?

You <u>hafta</u> know the rules of the culture.

F. Practice. (Audio)   People say short forms, but write the long forms. Listen to the conversation and write the long form of the words you hear.

A: Do you _____ _____ try bargaining in the market?
                                   1

B: You mean you're not _____ _____ pay the asking price?
                                         2

A: No way! You _____ _____ know the rules of the culture. C'mon . . . let's try it!
                             3

B: Uh h . . . I'm not sure . . .

A: Are you afraid? Well I'm not! I'm _____ _____ give it a try.
                                       4

Review: Language Functions

Asking for Confirmation and Confirming Understanding (Video/Audio)

Listen to these examples of how to ask for and offer confirmation. You'll use these functions in the next section.

Put It Together

Asking for Confirmation Pair

Student A chooses a topic from the following list and makes a statement about it. Student B asks a confirmation question. Student A answers Student B's question and tells the truth. Use tag questions. Remember to use correct intonation. Take turns playing the roles of Student A and Student B.

Examples: A: My favorite restaurant is Tandoori House.

B: You really like Indian food, don't you?

A: Yes, I do.

* * *

A: I saw the new Clint Eastwood movie last night.

B: Oh, you like Eastwood, don't you?

A: No, I don't.

Topics

- my favorite restaurant
- a movie I saw recently
- my favorite place to visit
- food for a holiday or celebration in my culture
- something interesting I learned about how to behave in a foreign country or culture

Part Four Broadcast English: Global Business Ethics

Before Listening

A. Thinking Ahead. Group   You are going to hear a radio program about global business ethics. **Ethics** is a system of behavior that people agree is good or right. Before you listen, test your business ethics. Read each situation and decide if you agree or disagree. Then share your answers with your group.

1. You want a government agency to hire your company to do a big project. It's OK to **bribe** someone who works for the agency (in other words, give him or her money or a gift) in order to get the project.

Agree   Disagree

2. You hire people for a big corporation. An important job is available in the company. Your brother needs work, but he isn't the most qualified candidate for this particular job. It's OK to hire him anyway because he is your brother.

Agree   Disagree

3. It's OK to tell a lie on your résumé in order to get a job that you really want.

Agree   Disagree

4. You are **competing** with another company for an important project. (In other words, you are both trying to get it at the same time.) It's OK to send a spy into the other company to learn information that will help you win the job instead of the other company.

Agree   Disagree

5. You are a manager. Your company has sent you to work in an office in another country. You work with a local manager who has the same title and job as you. The local manager gets more money than you do. This is fair.

Agree   Disagree

B. Predicting. Pair   Before you listen, make a prediction about what you are going to hear in the radio program. Discuss the answer to this question.

• Do you think different countries have different business ethics? Explain your answer.

C. Guessing Meaning from Context.   In the radio program, you are going to hear some words that may be new to you. Before you listen, guess the meaning of some of the words from the program. The words are underlined in the sentences. Look for clues to their meaning in the words around them.

Write your guess in the blank after each sentence. Then check your guess with your teacher or the dictionary.

1. Bob thought his competitor <u>unscrupulously</u> offered the government a bribe. However, offering bribes is an accepted practice in his competitor's country.

Guess: _____

2. Some companies have a <u>code of conduct</u>, and all employees, even managers, must behave according to these rules.

Guess: _____

3. How can companies help their employees to have <u>moral courage</u>, in other words, to be brave enough to do the right thing in business?

Guess: _____

4. In the United States, many industries have <u>lobbyists</u> to represent them in the government and help improve their business.

Guess: _____

5. A foreign businessperson tried to bribe Sue because she's an <u>insider</u>—she works for the company and he thought she would help him get the project.

Guess: _____

6. Before we sign a contract with a company, we go through <u>a due diligence process</u>—we learn important facts about it such as how much money it has, and how it does business.

Guess: _____

7. Everyone's talking about the government <u>scandal</u>. Apparently, an official took a bribe from a foreign company.

Guess: _____

8. Many Americans have a very <u>parochial</u> idea of what is right and what is wrong. But doing business globally is giving them a more international view of ethics.

Guess: _____

D. Vocabulary Preparation: Idioms and Phrasal Verbs.   There are many idiomatic expressions and phrasal verbs in the radio program. First, read each sentence and guess the meaning of the underlined words. Then choose their meaning from the definitions in the box. Write the letter in the blanks.

> **Definitions**
>
> *a.* get   *d.* stop employing
>
> *b.* be in a better situation   *e.* quit
>
> *c.* to force progress

Sentences

_____ **1.** We can't get the project this way; we need to bribe someone in order <u>to push</u> negotiations <u>along</u>.

_____ **2.** You would <u>be better off</u> if you told the truth on your résumé. Otherwise, you might get a job that you can't do.

_____ **3.** If the company doesn't have a good code of conduct, we will <u>walk away from</u> the project.

_____ **4.** American managers <u>rake in</u> a lot more money than managers in some other countries do.

_____ **5.** They are going to <u>lay off</u> some workers because there isn't enough work for them.

 academic Strategy

Finding a Culture Informant

Some expressions that you hear in American English refer to cultural things such as food, sports, and religion. For example, "The ball's in your court" refers to basketball, but it means "It's your turn to take action." People in the United States and Canada use many of these expressions in business discussions.

    These expressions are difficult to understand unless you have lived in the country for a long time. Therefore, it's a good idea to find an **informant**—a person (for example, a teacher or someone else in your school, or a neighbor) who knows the culture well. Ask him or her to explain expressions that you can't figure out.

E. Vocabulary Preparation: Expressions with Cultural References.   The radio program is about ethics. Therefore, some expressions refer to religion and **morals** (rules of behavior). There's also an expression that refers to sports. These might be difficult to understand. Look at the following expressions in context. If you are not sure what they mean, ask an informant.

1. We wouldn't have misunderstandings in international business if everyone followed <u>the Golden Rule</u>: Do unto others as you would have them do unto you.

2. Some of the talks at the business ethics conference sounded like <u>Sunday sermons</u>.

3. One of the speakers was a <u>Jesuit priest</u> who taught business courses at a university.

4. Jake didn't <u>play by the rules</u>, so his company fired him.

Listening

A. Listening for the Main Idea. (Audio)   Listen to the radio program. As you listen, try to answer this question:

• What was the purpose of the Code of Ethics conference?

 *listening* Strategy

Listening for Numerical Information (Audio)

Speakers often give important information as numbers or quantities. They use numbers and quantities to support their ideas. They often refer to quantities in percent. Listen carefully for numbers and other expressions such as "percent." Here is an example:

Over <u>30 percent</u> of our employees do not speak English as their first language.

B. Listening for Numerical Information. (Audio)   Listen to a part of the program. This time, listen for numerical information: numbers and percents. Write the numbers from the box in the correct places in the blanks.

> **Numbers**
>
> 200 (use twice)   30   86   billions

. . . American companies lose _____ of dollars each year in contracts because foreign
                                        1

competitors unscrupulously offer commissions or consultant fees and other sweeteners to help push

negotiations along in global markets. While _____ percent of American companies have codes
                                                    2

of conduct, for example, less than _____ percent of Japanese firms do. German companies
                                            3

aren't bound by the same laws against bribe-giving U.S. companies are. In Tokyo last weekend,

_____ business ethicists met for the first world conference. Marketplace's Jocelyn Ford reports.
        4

    Jocelyn Ford: When _____ of the world's experts of business ethics get together, some of
                                5

the topics sound like Sunday sermons.

listening Strategy

Listening for an Example   Audio

Speakers sometimes support their ideas by giving examples that explain their ideas or give more information about them. Examples are cases or situations that illustrate an idea. Sometimes (but not always), a speaker will introduce an example with an expression. Some of these expressions include the following:

- for example
- for instance

- such as
- an example (of this) is . . .

C. Listening for an Example.   Audio   Listen to other parts of the program. First, listen for an example about bribery. Write your answer in the blanks.

1. Example about bribery _____

2. Is bribery the same in all countries? Give an example that supports your answer.

_____

_____

_____

_____

_____

Now listen for an example that explains another important concept: fairness. Write your answer in the blanks.

3. Example about fairness _____

4. Is fairness the same in all countries? Give an example that supports your answer.

_____

_____

_____

_____

_____

After Listening

D. Discussion. (Group)   Discuss the answers to these questions.

1. Do different countries have different business ethics? Explain your answer.

2. What was the purpose of the Code of Ethics conference?

3. Is bribery the same in all countries? Give an example (from the program or one of your own) that supports your answer.

4. Is fairness the same in all countries? Give an example (from the program or one of your own) that supports your answer.

5. Have you ever had an experience with bribery? If so, tell your group members about it.

6. Give an example from your personal experience of an act that was unfair.

. . : : : : : **Part Five** Academic English: Ethics and Doing Business Internationally

Before Listening

A. Discussion. (Group)   You are going to listen to a lecture about doing global business. Before you listen, discuss the answers to these questions.

1. If someone said "no" right away when you were negotiating with him or her, would that seem polite or impolite to you?

2. How far apart do people stand in your culture when they discuss business? Stand up and demonstrate this to your group members.

3. How important are business cards in your culture? What do people do with them when they receive them? If you're not sure, take some small rectangular pieces of paper and pretend that they are business cards. Observe each other as you exchange them in a normal way for your culture. Are there any differences?

academic Strategy

Asking Questions Before You Listen

Before you listen to a lecture, it is a good idea to ask yourself questions about it. This helps you to think ahead so you can focus on the lecture.

B. Thinking Ahead. Look at the outline for the lecture on pages 28–29 and think about your discussion in Exercise A. What *don't* you know about doing business globally and the ethics of international business? Write at least three questions about the subject.

_____

_____

_____

C. Guessing Meaning from Context.   In the lecture, you are going to hear some words that may be new to you. Before you listen, guess the meaning of some of the words from the lecture. The words are underlined in the sentences. Look for clues to their meaning in the words around them.
   Write your guess in the blank after each sentence. Then check your guess with your teacher or the dictionary.

1. Doing business in a <u>homogeneous</u> culture is less complicated for people who live in that culture. Doing business within the United States, however, is more difficult because people from many different cultures work together.

    Guess: _____

2. The two companies had <u>prolonged</u> negotiations; they started in January and didn't end until June.

    Guess: _____

3. I was <u>suspicious</u> because he wouldn't look me in the eye while we were talking. I didn't think that he was telling me the truth.

    Guess: _____

4. You will be <u>charged</u> with theft; the police will officially blame you for stealing money from the company.

    Guess: _____

5. You can <u>deduct</u> business expenses from your income so your tax bill will be lower.

    Guess: _____

6. Some employees cannot <u>cope</u> with cultural differences. In fact, they have such a difficult time with them that they need to take training courses.

    Guess: _____

7. Tim was the company's <u>whistle-blower</u>—he called his manager every time he saw an employee behave unethically.

Guess: _____

8. When a manager does not behave ethically, it <u>undermines</u> a company's code of ethics because other employees may feel it is not necessary to follow the code either.

Guess: _____

Listening

A. Listening for the Main Idea. `Audio` Listen to the lecture one time. Don't take notes. Don't worry about understanding everything. Just listen for the main idea. As you listen, try to answer this question:

• What are some cultural differences in doing business internationally?

listening Strategy

Listening for the Meaning of New Words and Expressions `Audio`

Speakers have different ways of defining the terms that they use. One way that speakers present a definition is after the word *is*. Here is an example:

A code of conduct <u>is</u> a set of rules that a company establishes for all its employees.

Speakers sometimes also insert a definition right after the term, without any introductory word. These kinds of definitions are easy to see when you read, because they use punctuation. It's more difficult when you are listening, but if you listen carefully, you sometimes hear pauses where the punctuation would be. Here is an example:

A whistle-blower—a person who reports unethical behavior—has to be very careful about his or her own behavior.

B. Listening for the Meaning of New Words and Expressions. `Audio` Listen to these words and expressions in sentences from the lecture. Then write the definition that you hear.

1. culture = _____

2. personal distance = _____

listening Strategy

Taking Lecture Notes `Audio`

Questions on most college course exams are based on material from both the textbook and in-class lectures. So it's important to take good notes when you listen to a lecture. You'll practice lecture note taking in every chapter of this book. Here are a few suggestions for taking good notes:

- Don't "just listen." Taking notes makes you an active listener, which helps you remember information later.
- Don't try to write everything that you hear. Note taking is not dictation.
- Don't write complete sentences. Instead write key words. You can use abbreviations, too.

Example: The professor says: "In Japan, exchanging business cards is an important ritual."

You can write the following: Japan: exchanging bus. cards important

listening Strategy

Organizing Your Notes `Audio`

It's a good idea to take notes in an organized way. This helps you group related information. There are many ways to organize lecture notes, depending on the subject of the lecture. One of the most common ways is the formal outline. A formal outline distinguishes general ideas from specific ideas. In a formal outline, you write general ideas to the left, and indent specific ideas. You use symbols to indicate **levels of generality** (going from the most general ideas to the least general ideas): Roman numerals (I., II.), capital letters (A., B.), Arabic numerals (1., 2.), and lowercase letters (a., b.).

Example:

Types of Businesses in South Bay Island

  I. Manufacturing
    A. Clothing
      1. Women's
        a. Bodega Fashions
        b. Sausalito Sweaters
      2. Children's
        a. BabyBoots, Inc.
        b. Tot Togs

> B. Furniture
>> 1. Natural Woods, Inc.
>> 2. Chairs R Us
>
> II. Media
>> A. Video Production
>>> 1. Garnet Media, Inc.
>>> 2. AllSports Videos
>>
>> B. Publishing
>>> 1. Newspapers
>>>> a. *South Bay Island Times*
>>>> b. *South Bay Advertiser*
>>>
>>> 2. Magazines
>>>> a. *What's New?*
>>>> b. *Marine Quarterly*

C. Taking Notes: Using an Outline. **Audio**   Listen to the lecture and fill in as much of the outline as you can. Start at the beginning. Write your notes in the blanks. Don't worry if you can't fill in much. You'll listen to the lecture again.

Ethics and Doing Business Internationally

I. Introduction

   A definition of culture: _a set of beliefs and values that the members_
   of a particular society commonly share

II. One Area of Difference: Saying "No"

   A. Japanese example: _____

   _____

   _____

   B. American example: _____

   _____

   _____

III. Another Area of Difference: Personal Distance

   A. Definition: _____

   _____

    B. Japanese and Latin American example: _____

    _____

    _____

    C. American example: _____

    _____

    _____

IV. Another Area of Difference: Business Cards

    A. Japanese example: _____

    _____

    B. American example: _____

    _____

V. Differences in Ethical Behavior

    A. Bribery

        1. In the United States bribery is _____

        2. Examples in Europe

            a. Spain: _____

            b. Germany: _____

            c. Russia: _____

VI. How Companies Handle Ethical Issues

    A. Have a "code of ethics." This is (definition):

    _____

    B. Have "whistle-blower" laws. They are:

    _____

    _____

    C. Train employees in:

        1. _____

        2. _____

    D. Encourage ethical behavior by making sure _____ behave ethically

    E. Think _____ , act _____

listening Strategy

Listening for Differences   Audio

Speakers use certain expressions to tell you that a different example is coming. These expressions introduce a contrast between two ideas or examples. Here are some of these expressions:

- On the other hand

- However

Example: The Japanese take business cards very seriously and spend a lot of time examining them. <u>However,</u> Americans just put them into their pockets as soon as they receive them.

D. Taking Notes: Listening for Differences.   Audio   Listen again to the lecture. Fill in more of the outline. This time, pay particular attention to the differences in the examples from different countries. Focus on the examples of bribery in Europe. Make sure that you complete this section with examples (Section V A, Items 2a through 2c).

After Listening

Using Your Notes.   Use your notes to discuss the answers to these questions about the lecture.

1. What are some cultural differences in doing business internationally?

2. Can you think of additional differences in doing business internationally?

3. How does the idea of bribery differ from one culture to another?

4. How do some companies in the United States help employees to cope with cultural differences in doing business? Do you think these actions really work? Do you have any other (or better) ideas?

5. Do you want to work overseas (or with people from different cultures)? Why or why not?

Step Beyond

Giving a Presentation. **Group**   You are going to **collaborate** (work together) in a small group to give a presentation. The presentation is on "How Our Company Copes with Cultural Differences in Business Ethics."

Step One

Get into groups of three or four. Try to have both males and females and people from different cultures in your group. You and your partners have a business. You have employees from different countries and cultures, and you send employees overseas to do business. First, decide the following and take notes on your decisions:

- a type of business
- a name for your business
- what country your business is located in
- what countries you do business with
- how many employees you have and where they come from

 speaking Strategy

Taking Turns

When you collaborate in a group, it's important to take turns talking. If you like to talk, make sure to give the quieter group members a chance to speak. You can help them by asking them for their opinions. If you don't like to talk, force yourself to make at least one comment. If you are shy, sometimes it helps to write down your ideas first, and then say them.

Then decide how you will cope with cultural differences. Decide which of the following your company will have. Also, decide how you will put them into action. Again, take notes on your ideas.

- A code of ethics. If you have this, what is your code? Write a list of rules for employees. Say which employees must follow it. (All? Or just the lower-level employees?)
- A toll-free telephone number so employees can report unethical behavior. If you choose this, explain what will happen when an employee reports on someone.
- Cultural training classes. If you decide to give classes, describe them: What will you teach? Who will take the classes?
- Think of your own ways to solve problems.

Step Two

Now present your company to the rest of the class. Describe your company and explain how you plan to help your employees cope with cultural differences. Use your notes.

chapter Two

International Economy

In this chapter, you'll listen to and discuss information about economic systems in different countries and how these countries take care of their citizens.

Part One Introduction: Welfare-to-Work in San Francisco

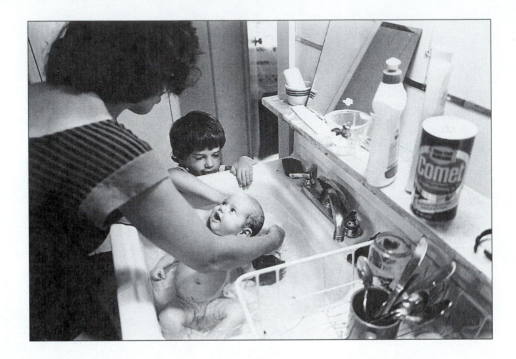

A. Brainstorming. `Pair`   Read the following situation. Then, with your partner, brainstorm for ideas on how Sharon can improve her situation.

Sharon's Story

Sharon is a single mother with **pre-school-aged** (three or four years old) children who lives in a big city in the United States. She has received **welfare** (money from the government for living expenses) all her life; her mother received welfare when she was growing up. Sharon has a high school education, but did not

5   go to college. She has few job skills; for example, she has never used a computer. Before, the government gave her money to support her family. Now, she can receive money only if she finds a job, and she can receive the money for only two more years. She's afraid of what will happen to her children when the government money stops. She's depressed because she can't support her family—she feels like a failure.

B. Reading.   Read the following passage about welfare in a U.S. city. As you read, try to answer this question:

• How has the welfare system in the United States changed?

Welfare in a U.S. City

In 1996 President Clinton signed a new welfare **bill** (a proposal for a law) that changed the welfare system in the United States. The new system is called "Welfare-to-Work." Before
5 1996, parents who did not have jobs received checks from the government to pay for their living expenses. They could receive this support money for many years. In the new system, parents can continue to get benefits if they look for
10 and find a job. Additionally, they can receive government money for only two years in a row and for only five years in their entire lives.

This new system requires city welfare departments to make big changes. Before, they sim-
15 ply issued checks to people. Now they must offer training and find jobs for people. And because some of these people have never worked before, they have to start in **low-skill level jobs**.

How is this system working in one major
20 U.S. city, San Francisco? At the end of 1998, San Francisco had two years to get jobs for about 7,000 **welfare recipients** (people who receive welfare). The city is in a good position because it has one of the highest numbers of low-skill
25 level jobs in the country, with more than one low-skill job for every low-skill job **seeker** (a person who looks for a job). On the other hand, New York City has five people looking for every low-skill job. San Francisco also has an energetic and
30 involved business community: it has given a great deal of time and money to developing several job-training programs. One of the most successful of these **corporate-sponsored** programs (a program paid for by companies) is San Fran-
35 cisco Works. SF Works started with $7 million in funding and promised to find jobs for 2,000 welfare recipients by the year 2000.

Anita Meyers-Green is one of SF Works' success stories. The former welfare recipient and
40 mother of seven now works in an office at the University of California, San Francisco hospital. She earns $12 an hour. She's at her job by 7:30 each morning, after she gets her children ready for school.

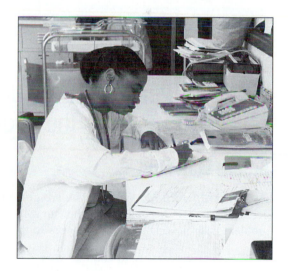

45   "We all get up at 4 in the morning," she says. "I couldn't work if I was worried my youngest was wearing two different socks or somebody forgot their lunch . . . . I'm proud to be working . . . . I'm so glad I got this chance, and I just hope
50 it's available to more women who need it."

C. Discussion. (Group)   Discuss the answers to these questions.

1. How has the welfare system in the United States changed?

2. What is the new responsibility of city welfare departments?

3. Why might the welfare-to-work system be successful in San Francisco?

4. What are some of the challenges a person such as Anita may face?

5. How does Anita feel about herself?

6. Which do you think is better for an unemployed mother: to receive welfare checks or to get help finding a job?

D. Response Writing.   Choose *one* of these topics. Write about it for ten minutes. Don't worry about grammar and don't use a dictionary. Just put as many ideas as you can on paper.

• Discuss your answer to this question: How should a government help poor women with children?

• Discuss your opinion of the welfare-to-work program. Do you think it is a good idea? Why or why not?

• Compare the U.S. welfare-to-work system with the welfare system of another country.

. . : : : : **Part Two** Everyday English: Help for the Poor (Interview)

Before Listening

A. Thinking Ahead. (Group)   You are going to listen to Evan interview people on the street. He's going to ask them for opinions on how to solve the problem of poverty. Before you listen, discuss this problem in groups. Discuss the answers to these questions.

1. What is the best way to help the poor?

2. Who should be responsible for helping the poor? The government? Religious groups? Private organizations?

Write your ideas on a piece of paper. Then choose the best one.

B. Comparing Ideas. (Class)   Share your best idea with the other groups. Did anyone have the same idea?

speaking Strategy

Predicting

When you say something that you are not completely sure of, you are making a prediction. To show your listeners that you are not completely sure about an idea, you can introduce it with an expression such as the following:

- I think (that) . . .
- I imagine (that) . . .

Examples: I think that most people will say that the government should improve education.

I imagine most people will say that the government should improve education.

C. Predicting. **Group**   You are going to listen to seven people. They give their opinion on what the government should do to help the poor. What do you think that most people will say? In your group, make predictions.

D. Vocabulary Preparation.   The people in the interview use some words and expressions that may be new to you. First, read each sentence and guess the meaning of the underlined words. Then choose their meaning from the definitions in the box. Write the letter in the blanks.

Sentences

_____ **1.** The purpose of a job training program is to get people back on their feet so they can take care of themselves.

_____ **2.** Some people would rather take a do-it-yourself approach to improving their lives instead of accepting welfare.

_____ **3.** He said that he didn't want a handout; instead, he wanted a job that paid him enough money to feed his family.

_____ **4.** SF Works helps people who live in San Francisco. It's an example of welfare-to-work at the local level.

_____ **5.** Job training helps people get off welfare.

_____ **6.** Government programs have to make provisions for childcare for working mothers because it is very expensive.

Definitions

a. provide; offer

b. stop receiving

c. without help

d. help make someone strong, independent, and able to care for him- or herself

e. money someone gives without expecting to get it back

f. local government, usually city government

Listening

A. Listening for the Main Idea. **Video/Audio**   Now listen to the interview. Listen for the answer to this question and circle the letter of the correct answer.

- What solution do most people have to the problem?

    a. The government should help poor people help themselves.

    b. The poor should help themselves without government help.

B. Listening for Details. **Video/Audio**   Now listen again. Which speakers think that the government should create programs (for example, education and job training) to help the poor? Which speakers think that the government is not the solution? Which speakers have a different answer? Put a check (✓) in the boxes.

Speaker Number	The Government Should Help	The Government Won't Solve the Problem	Different Solution
1	✓		
2			
3			
4			
5			
6			
7			

C. Listening for Specific Ideas. (Video/Audio)   Listen again to some of the speakers. Listen for the
answers to these questions.

1. Speaker 2: What does she think is wrong with giving people handouts?

_____

_____

_____

2. Speaker 4: What does he say we need instead of government programs?

_____

_____

_____

3. Speaker 6: Where does she think we need to improve schools?

_____

_____

_____

4. Speaker 7: What concern does this woman have about working mothers?

_____

_____

_____

After Listening

A. Conducting an Interview. Group   Interview three students in your class. Ask them for their opinions on how to solve the problem of poverty. Write their answers in the chart.

Student Name	Student 1 _____	Student 2 _____	Student 3 _____
1. What is the best way to help the poor, in your opinion?			
2. Why do you think this is the best way?			
3. If possible, give an example of an organization, program, or government that helps the poor in this way.			

B. Reporting Interview Results. Group   Form small groups. Try not to be in a group with someone that you interviewed. Report and discuss the results of your interview. Try to answer these questions:

1. Did students suggest any one solution more than another?

2. Do most people think that the government should help the poor?

3. What other solutions did students have?

4. What examples of successful programs or governments did students give?

.. .: :| | **Part Three** The Mechanics of Listening and Speaking

Language Functions

Asking for Permission **Audio**

When you ask a stranger for permission to do something, you usually use polite, formal language.

Here are some formal examples:

- May I ask you a question?
- Do you mind if I ask you a question?
- Would you mind if I asked you a question?

Grammar Note: When you use "Would" (instead of "Do"), the verb in the *if*-clause is in the past tense.

You can use slightly less formal language if the situation is less formal, and/or the strangers are your **peers** (people just like you). Less formal situations might include being in class or at a party.

Here are some less formal examples:

- Can I ask you a question?
- Could I borrow your pen?

Giving and Refusing Permission (Audio)

When you want to give permission, your answer can be formal or informal, depending on the situation. You answer honestly. Notice some ways to say "no" politely. You can add an excuse when you say "no."

Here are some formal examples:

May I ask you a question?

Yes	No
Certainly.	No, I'm sorry.
Of course.	I'm sorry. I'd rather you didn't.
	No, I don't have the time.

Here are some less formal examples:

Can I ask you a question?

Yes	No
Sure.	Get lost!
Go right ahead.	Sorry, no!
Shoot.*	No way!

*Shoot = Go right ahead.

A. Practice. (Audio) Listen to Student A's request for permission. Read the cue and give an appropriate answer.

Examples: A: Can I ask you a question? (Yes)

   B: Sure.

   A: May I sit here? (No)

   B: Sorry, my friend's joining me any minute.

1. (Yes) B: _____

2. (No) B: _____

3. (No) B: _____

4. (Yes) B: _____

5. (Yes) B: _____

Language Function

Answering Do/Would you mind . . . ? ⬤Audio

Notice these questions:

- Do you mind* if I ask you a question?

- Would you mind if I asked you a question?

People often use "Do/Would you mind . . . ?" when they want permission to ask you a question.

You can answer these questions honestly. If it's OK for the person to ask you a question, you answer

- No, not at all.

This means, "No, I don't mind. You can ask the question."

If you *do* mind, you might answer

- Sorry, I don't have time.

  Example: Do you mind if I smoke?

In this case, you might answer

- No, I don't mind.

- No, go right ahead.

OR:

- Yes, I do. I'm allergic to smoke.

- Please don't. I'm allergic to smoke.

*Mind = object to something.

B. Practice. (Audio)   Listen to these questions. Read the cue and give an appropriate answer.

Examples: A: Do you mind if I smoke? (Yes)

B: Yes, I do. It makes me sick.

A: Do you mind if I smoke? (No)

B: No, go right ahead.

1. (Yes) B: _____

_____

2. (No) B: _____

_____

3. (No) B: _____

_____

4. (Yes) B: _____

_____

5. (Yes) B: _____

_____

C. Practice. (Pair)   Practice refusing permission and adding excuses to the following questions.

Example: A: May I sit here?

B: Sorry, I'm waiting for my friend.

1. A: May I sit here?

B: No, sorry, _____

2. A: Do you mind if I smoke?

B: Yes, _____

3. A: Would you mind if I asked you a question?

B: Sorry, _____

4. A: Could I borrow your pen?

    B: No, sorry, _____

5. A: May I borrow your umbrella?

    B: No, sorry, _____

Intonation

Yes/No Questions Audio

When you ask a question that has "yes" or "no" as an answer, your voice goes up at the end. This is rising intonation. Here are some examples:

Can I ask you a question?   Do you mind if I smoke?

When you make a statement, your voice always goes down at the end. This is falling intonation. Here are some examples:

Go right ahead.   I'm allergic to smoke.

D. Practice. Audio Practice rising and falling intonation. Listen to the speaker. Repeat the statements and questions. Make sure your voice goes up if you hear a *yes/no* question and down if you hear a statement.

Pronunciation

Reduced Forms in Questions With -d + you Audio

When people speak naturally, some words (and combinations of sounds) become *reduced,* or short. Here are some examples of short forms in questions with *you:*

Long Form	Short Form
Would you mind if I sat here?	Wouldja mind if I sat here?
Could you understand him?	Couldja understand him?
Did you know her very well?	Didja know her very well?

People usually *say* the reduced form but *write* the long form. (The reduced form is not correct in formal writing.)

E. Practice. Audio   Listen to the conversation and write the long form of the words you hear.

1. _____ help me with this problem?

2. _____ read the last chapter?

3. _____ mind if I asked you a question?

4. _____ hear what I just said?

5. _____ put out that cigarette, please?

Review: Language Functions

Asking for Permission to Ask a Question and Offering Permission Video/Audio

Listen to these examples of how Evan asks for permission and how people respond to him. You'll use these functions in the next section.

Put It Together

Asking and Answering Questions for Permission

Practice. Pair   Ask and answer questions for permission. Take turns playing the roles of Student A and Student B. Follow the cues in the boxes. Remember to use rising intonation for *yes/no* questions.

Student A

1. You are sitting next to Student B on a campus bench. Ask if you can smoke.
2. The cafeteria is crowded. You see one empty seat at Student B's table. Ask if you can sit there.
3. You have to do an interview for a class assignment. Ask Student B if you can ask a question.
4. You are at a party. Student B looks interesting. Ask Student B if you can ask a question. Try to find out Student B's name.
5. Class is starting. You forgot to bring a pen. Ask Student B if you can borrow a pen.

Student B

When Student A asks you a question, you

1. Refuse permission and give an excuse.
2. Give permission.
3. Refuse permission and give an excuse.
4. First refuse permission. Then change your mind.
5. Refuse permission and give an excuse.

Example: A: May I ask you a question?

B: Sorry. I'm in a hurry.

. . : : ! !   **Part Four** Broadcast English: Welfare Systems in Russia, Canada, and Germany

Before Listening

A. Thinking Ahead. Group   You are going to hear a radio program about welfare systems in three countries: Russia, Canada, and Germany. Before you listen, share any information you have about these countries in your groups. First, discuss the answers to these questions.

1. What do you know about the economic systems of these countries?

2. What do you know about the welfare systems of these countries?

3. What changes have these countries experienced in the last ten or twenty years?

B. Predicting. Pair   Before you listen, make a prediction about what you are going to hear. Discuss the answer to this question with your partner.

• Do you think that social welfare in Russia, Canada, and/or Germany is **adequate**? (In other words, is there enough welfare to help people who need it?) Explain your answer.

C. Guessing Meaning from Context.   Before you listen to the radio program, guess the meaning of some of the words from the program. The words are underlined in the sentences. Look for clues to their meaning in the words around them.

Write your guess in the blank after each sentence. Then check your guess with your teacher or the dictionary.

1. In 1996 President Clinton signed a welfare <u>reform</u> bill that resulted in great changes in the welfare system in the United States.

Guess: _____

2. Uncle Nikolai is a <u>pensioner</u>. His income comes from money that the government gave him when he stopped working.

Guess: _____

3. Paul Newman is a <u>philanthropist</u>. His food products earn millions of dollars every year, and he gives all the money to charities that help people in need.

Guess: _____

4. The government is experiencing a <u>deficit</u>—it's spending more money than it's taking in.

Guess: _____

5. The government <u>concocted</u> a plan to change the welfare program, but the system that it created didn't work.

Guess: _____

6. If we follow the <u>budget</u> that we created, we'll always know how much money we have coming in and going out.

Guess: _____

7. Because the government is experiencing a deficit, it's going to have to <u>cut the budget</u>. That means that there will be less money for welfare.

Guess: _____

8. We have enough money in the budget, so we don't have to <u>skimp</u> on extras such as travelling and buying new clothes.

Guess: _____

9. In a <u>welfare state</u> such as Sweden, people receive help from the government for all of their needs from birth to death.

Guess: _____

D. Vocabulary Preparation: Idioms and Phrasal Verbs. There are many idiomatic expressions and phrasal verbs in the radio program. How many of them do you know? First, read each sentence and guess the meaning of the underlined words. Then choose their meaning from the definitions in the box. Write the letter in the blanks.

Sentences

_____ 1. We are <u>wrestling with</u> how to improve our economic situation: Should we try to find higher paying jobs or spend less money?

_____ 2. If we <u>cut costs</u>, we'll be able to go on a vacation next year.

_____ 3. I had a hard time <u>making ends meet</u> when I lost my job, so I asked my mother to loan me some money.

_____ 4. I was <u>at the end of my tether</u>: I was completely out of money and didn't know what to do.

_____ 5. I asked for a loan only <u>as a last resort</u> after I had tried to find another solution.

_____ 6. Both candidates were <u>front-runners</u> in the last election because both had good ideas about welfare reform.

_____ 7. Everyone supported welfare reform, so the smart candidates used it as a <u>trump card</u> to win the last election.

Definitions

a. ahead of other people in a competition or an election

b. having difficulty making a decision about

c. something that gives a person an advantage in a competition

d. having enough money

e. spend less money

f. the last action to take after trying everything else

g. unable to tolerate a bad situation

Listening

A. Listening for the Main Idea. **Audio** Listen to the radio program. As you listen, try to answer this question:

- Are the welfare systems of Russia, Canada, and Germany adequate?

Russian pensioners

The high cost of medicine in Canada

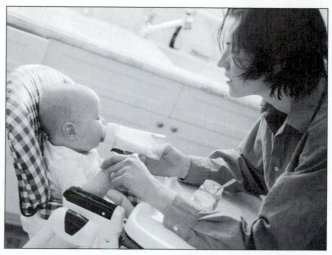

A single, unemployed mother in Germany

B. Listening for Details. **Audio**   Listen to parts of the radio program. This time, listen for the answers to these questions.

1. Do people in Russia feel that welfare reform is an improvement?

_____

2. Why did Canada have to cut welfare assistance?

_____

_____

_____

3. What does a welfare recipient in Germany receive?

_____

_____

_____

listening Strategy

Understanding the Passive Voice Audio

People sometimes use the passive voice when they discuss social science subjects (such as economics and politics). The passive voice is not commonly used in colloquial English. However, it's important to understand it when you hear or read it. Passive sentences are often difficult to understand because their focus is different: The object of the active sentence is in the subject position in the passive sentence because it is more important, and the subject (called the "agent") of the active sentence is sometimes missing in the passive. It is easier to understand passive sentences if you can tell the difference between who is doing the action and who (or what) is receiving the action.

Compare a passive voice sentence with an active voice sentence:

Active

| Most people | consider | welfare programs | a last resort. |
| Subject (Agent) | Verb | Object (Receiver of action) | |

Passive

| Welfare programs | are still considered | a last resort. |
| Receiver of action | Verb | |

The subject of the verb "consider" in the active sentence is missing in the passive sentence because it is unimportant. (Notice also how the verb changes in the passive sentence.)

Sometimes the speaker states the subject of the verb (the agent) of the active sentence in a passive sentence using a "by" phrase. Here is an example:

| Welfare reforms | have been seen | by many people | as a threat. |
| Receiver of action | Verb | Agent | |

C. Listening for the Passive Voice. Audio   Listen again to other parts of the radio program. You will hear passive statements. Listen for the answers to these questions.

1. Who used social welfare as a trump card during the recent election in Russia?

_____

2. Who once **financed** (paid money for) benefits in Germany such as medical cures in a spa?

_____

D. *Listening for Numbers.* (Audio) Numbers are important in discussions of economics. Now listen carefully to a part of the radio program. Fill in the blanks as you listen. Then answer the questions and circle the letter of the correct answer.

Critics have called upon the Quebec government to abandon this plan, saying the consequences could be disastrous, with poor people skimping on the medication they need. Approximately

_____ of the province's _____ residents are on welfare. That amounts to
      1   2

almost _____ individuals dependent on government assistance. The government's in-
                  3

come security program provides Quebecers with up to _____ Canadian dollars per month.
                                                                 4

That's approximately _____ dollars U.S., depending on their status. But the welfare
                                  5

programs are still considered a last resort.

Questions

1. Approximately how many of Quebec's residents are on welfare?

 a. 100,000

 b. 8,000

 c. 800,000

2. Which number expression shows the portion of all of Quebec residents who are on welfare?

 a. 1 in 6

 b. 1 in 7

 c. 7 in 1

3. How many U.S. dollars does 800 Canadian dollars equal?

 a. 6

 b. 60

 c. 600

After Listening

A. Discussion. Group   Discuss the answers to these questions.

1. How has welfare in Russia changed since the **breakup** (end) of the Soviet Union?

2. How does Russia provide for the poor today?

3. Why did the Canadian government have to cut welfare assistance?

4. What kinds of things can a welfare recipient in Germany get from the government?

5. Are the welfare systems of Russia, Canada, and Germany good or bad, in your opinion?

B. Brainstorming: Designing a Welfare System. Group   In small groups, discuss the answer to this question.

• What services and other types of financial support should all citizens receive from their government?

. : : : : : Part Five Academic English: Social Welfare in Sweden and France

Before Listening

A. Discussion. Group   You are going to listen to a lecture about welfare systems in two more countries. Before you listen, discuss the answers to these questions in your groups.

1. Which countries have the best welfare systems, in your opinion? What makes them the best?

2. Which have the worst? What makes them the worst?

3. Which countries are now (or were in the past) welfare states?

4. What are some of the advantages of living in a welfare state?

5. Are there any disadvantages to living in a welfare state? What are they?

B. Thinking Ahead.
Look at the outlines for the lecture on pages 57–61. What *don't* you know about the economies of Sweden and France? What don't you know about the welfare systems of these countries? Write at least two questions about the subject.

_____

_____

_____

_____

C. Guessing Meaning from Context.
In the lecture, you are going to hear some words that may be new to you. Before you listen, guess the meaning of some words from the lecture. The words are underlined in the sentences. Look for clues to their meaning in the words around them.

Write your guess in the blank after each sentence. Then check your guess with your teacher or the dictionary.

1. The government of Xenrovia <u>redistributed</u> everyone's income so that now there are no very rich or very poor people; everyone earns about the same amount of money.

   Guess: _____

2. Xenrovia has <u>nurtured</u> small businesses by giving them money and special advantages to help them grow and become successful.

   Guess: _____

3. Because cigarette companies lowered the prices of their products to encourage <u>consumption</u>, they sold more cigarettes this year than last year.

   Guess: _____

4. Some people are not ready to study for professional jobs, so they have <u>vocational training</u> instead.

   Guess: _____

5. The new welfare reform bill is truly <u>innovative</u>; we've never seen one like it before.

   Guess: _____

6. The Xenrovia government is very involved in the economy. In fact, because it <u>intervenes</u> in economic matters, it can provide a lot of social welfare services to its citizens.

   Guess: _____

D. Vocabulary Preparation: Economic Terms.   Match these economic terms with their definitions. Write the letters in the blanks. If necessary, use a dictionary.

Economic Terms

_____ **1.** free enterprise

_____ **2.** the private sector

_____ **3.** industrial base

_____ **4.** incentives

_____ **5.** subsidies

_____ **6.** nationalization

_____ **7.** inflation

_____ **8.** recession

_____ **9.** revenue

Definitions

a. money that governments give to organizations to help make prices lower or make it cheaper to produce goods

b. things (usually money) that encourage people to work harder or produce more

c. a government taking control of a business

d. a period when there is less buying and selling of goods

e. doing business without much government control

f. businesses that are not controlled by the government

g. the presence of factories and large businesses in a country

h. money coming in

i. the rise in prices usually when the cost of producing goods increases

Listening

A. Listening for Main Ideas.   (Audio)   Listen to the lecture (in two parts) about the welfare systems in Sweden and France. Don't take notes. Don't worry about understanding everything. Just listen for the main ideas of the part. As you listen to Part One, try to answer this question:

• How does Sweden **equalize income** (make salaries equal)?

Now listen to Part Two. As you listen, try to answer this question:

• How did France improve its economy after World War II?

B. Taking Notes: Part One. (Audio) Listen to Part One of the lecture and fill in as much of the outline as you can. Start at the beginning. Don't worry if you can't fill in much. You'll listen to the lecture again.

Part One: Social Welfare in Sweden

I. The Swedish Economy

   A. Type of economy: _____ *welfare state* _____ or _____

   B. History:

      1. Swed. combined _____ and

         _____ to redistribute income

      2. after WWI, Swed. _____

         _____

      3. at the same time, Swed. has nurtured _____

         _____

C. Swedes believe in _____

_____

II. The Five Components for Equalizing Income in Sweden

    A. 1st component: Protects people from ups and downs of business cycles and unemployment

       1. govt. offers _____ and

          _____

       2. ensures wages for _____ and tax revenue

          for _____

    B. 2nd component: Allows private ownership and control over production

       1. no govt. involvement in _____ or

          _____

       2. Swed. dependent on _____

       3. Swed. markets unregulated = _____

          _____

    C. 3rd component: Wage policy: reduces difference between highest and lowest paid workers

       1. unions negotiate: _____

       2. unions also negotiate: _____

    D. 4th component: Policies ensure full employment and increase mobility of labor

       1. Swed. work ethic + employment programs = _____

          _____

       2. vocational training for _____

          _____

       3. subsidies for _____

          _____

    E. 5th component: Corrects problems of other four

       1. ex.: _____

          _____

       2. ex.: _____

          _____

III. Swedes Happy with System

   A. Swed. has achieved more _____

   _____ than many other economies

   B. Result: _____

   _____

   C. However, Swed. must _____

   _____ because

   _____

academic Strategy

Using Abbreviations in Note Taking   **Audio**

Notice the abbreviations and symbols in the notes on the Swedish economy.

ex.	example
4	four (or any number)
+	and
=	is, equals, results in

You can make up abbreviations and symbols as long as *you* understand them.

Practice.   Listen to these words and expressions. Try using your own abbreviations or symbols:

France	_____	government	_____
economy	_____	international	_____
to (as in 1950 <u>to</u> 1960)	_____	established	_____
World War I	_____	percent	_____
World War II	_____	less than	_____

C. Taking Notes: Part Two. (Audio)   Now listen to Part Two of the lecture and fill in as much of the outline as you can. Start at the beginning. Don't worry if you can't fill in much. You'll listen to the lecture again. Practice using abbreviations and symbols.

Part Two: Social Welfare in France

I. The French Economy

    A. Type of economy: _____Guided Market Economy_____ means:

    _____

    B. History

        1. situation after WWII: _____

        _____

        2. situation motivated French to develop policies that favored

        _____, _____,

        and _____: allows modernization and change

    C. Major theme of French industrial policy: govt. plays role

        1. areas: _____ and _____

        2. economy more international + European Union membership =

        _____

II. Periods in French Economy

    A. From late 1950s–early 1980s

        1. subsidies for these industries: _____,

        _____, and _____

        2. after industries were established, gave attention to

        _____

        _____

        3. this resulted in ability to _____

    B. Since late 1980s

        1. focus on _____

        _____

        2. competitive disinflation = _____

        _____

3. less successful due to _____

_____

C. Since early 1990s

1. econ. problems = election of _____

_____

2. current ideas: less _____ and

_____

III. Examples of French Welfare System

A. Budget deficit growing because: _____

_____

B. Childcare: _____

C. Tuition: _____

D. Extra pay: _____

E. When worker loses job: _____

_____

F. When a family member dies: _____

_____

listening **Strategy**

Guessing Meaning from Context (Audio)

Speakers have different ways of giving definitions of new terms. One way speakers present a definition is after the expression *that is*. Here is an example:

Xenrovia gives <u>subsidies</u> to new industries, <u>that is</u>, money to help make it cheaper to produce goods.

Another way is to repeat the term and its definition in a following sentence. Here is an example:

Xenrovia is currently experiencing a period of <u>inflation</u>. <u>Inflation</u> is a situation that occurs when prices increase, usually because the cost of producing goods increases.

D. Guessing Meaning from Context. (Audio)   Listen to these sentences from the lecture. You will hear the speaker give definitions of two terms. What does each term mean? Write your guess.

1. mobility of labor = _____

_____

2. competitive disinflation = _____

_____

listening Strategy

Using a Quotation to Illustrate an Idea (Audio)

Speakers sometimes quote material from experts to illustrate an idea that they are discussing. This is a way of defining a term, but it is very indirect. You need to listen carefully and think about how the quotation relates to the term. One way to do this is to write down the term and take notes on the quotation. When you take notes on the quotation, paraphrase it; that is, write it in your own words. Then look at your notes later and think about how the quotation explains the term.

E. Using a Quotation to Illustrate an Idea. (Audio)   Listen to a part of the lecture that contains a quotation. The quotation illustrates the term *jamlikhet*. First, paraphrase the quotation as you listen to it. Then read your notes. After that, try to guess the meaning of *jamlikhet*. Write your guess.

Notes:

_____

_____

_____

_____

jamlikhet probably means _____

_____

_____

listening **Strategy**

Listening for Causes and Effects `Audio`

When speakers discuss economics, they often talk about the effects of actions, plans, and policies. It's important to know the difference between the cause of something, and its effect or result. Here are some expressions that introduce causes:

- **because of**

    We have to pay more for goods and services   <u>because of</u> inflation.
                          effect   cause

- **due to**

    We have to pay more for goods and services   <u>due to</u> inflation.
                          effect   cause

Here are some expressions that introduce effects:

- **as a result**

    We are experiencing inflation.   <u>As a result</u>, we have to pay more for goods and services.
          cause   effect

- **result (-s, -ed) in**

    Inflation has   <u>resulted in</u> higher prices.
        cause   effect

- **the result is (that)**

    We are experiencing inflation.   <u>The result is that</u> now we have higher prices.
          cause   effect

F. Listening for Causes and Effects. `Audio` Listen to some information from the lecture. Listen for expressions that introduce causes and effects. Then answer the questions.

1. Why do many countries in the world envy Sweden?

_____

_____

2. Why can Swedish businesses be competitive in the international economy?

_____

_____

3. The Swedes are happy with their system. What is the result of this?

_____

_____

4. Why is France's budget deficit growing rapidly?

_____

_____

After Listening

Using Your Notes. Pair   Use your notes to discuss the answers to these questions about the lecture.

1. What kind of economy does Sweden have?

2. What are some policies that help Sweden to equalize salaries for its citizens?

3. How do the people of Sweden feel about their welfare system?

4. How did France improve its economy after World War II?

5. What caused the election of a new conservative government in France in the 1990s?

6. What are some examples of social insurance and welfare in France today?

7. Would you like to live in a country with a welfare system like Sweden's or France's? Which kind of welfare system would you prefer?

Step **Beyond**

Giving a Presentation. **Group**   You have read and listened to information about welfare systems in six countries: The United States, Russia, Canada, Germany, Sweden, and France. Now you are going to collaborate with a small group to give a presentation on welfare. The presentation is entitled "What a Government Should Provide for Its Citizens." To prepare for the presentation, use the notes that you have from the radio program and the brainstorming activity in Part Four, and the lecture notes from Part Five of this chapter.

Step One

Form groups of three or four. You and your partners will give a presentation on what a government should provide its citizens. Try to agree on items that a government can or should provide, such as the following:

- education
- healthcare
- childcare
- housing
- employment
- job training

Add items of your own.

Then, for each item, talk about any conditions it has, such as the following:

- how long the government will provide it
- to whom the government will provide it
- whether it should be completely free, or subsidized (it's not free, but the government helps to pay for it)

Add conditions of your own.

speaking **Strategy**

Compromising

You might have a very different opinion about a subject than your group members do. However, when you collaborate in a group, you must agree on things in order to accomplish the task. Therefore, it is often necessary to **compromise**. In other words, two or more people with different ideas might have to combine those ideas to make a new one that is less extreme than the original ones.

Example: You and your group need to finish a class assignment by a certain time. You don't have time to argue, so you need to *compromise* in order to finish the task faster.

You will also explain *why* a government should provide these items. Look at the examples in the following chart. Use the chart (or one like it) to plan your presentation. Your teacher will give you a time limit in which to finish the chart. Practice compromising to save time.

Should a Government Provide . . . ?	Yes	No	Reason
Education How many years? Completely free? Subsidized?			
Healthcare Completely free? Subsidized?			
Childcare How many years? Completely free? Subsidized?			
Housing			
Employment			
Job Training			
Your Ideas:			
Your Ideas:			
Your Ideas:			

speaking **Strategy**

Eye Contact

When you give a presentation in class, make eye contact with your audience. Look at the faces of the people you are speaking to. If you are speaking to a big group, move your eyes around the room to look at everyone. Don't keep your eyes on just one member of the audience.

Step Two

Now present your ideas to the class. Describe what the ideal government should provide its citizens and explain why you think these items are important. If possible, divide your presentation into parts so each member of your group can present one part.

As you listen to each other's presentations, take notes. Ask questions about each other's ideas.

unit

2

Art

chapter Three

Themes and Purposes

In this chapter, you'll listen to and discuss information about modern art. You'll also talk about art, artists, and the processes they follow when they create their art.

Part One Introduction: Art and Artists

A. Thinking Ahead. `Pair`   Talk about art with your partner. Discuss the answers to these questions.

1. What kinds of art do you like? Discuss types of art (or **media**) such as painting, sculpture, graphic art, and photography. You can also discuss **art periods** such as ancient art, Renaissance art, and modern art. Or you can talk about **art styles** such as impressionist art and surrealist art.

2. What is the purpose of posters, usually? Are posters "real" art, in your opinion?

B. Predicting. `Group`   You are going to read about an artist, Michael Cassidy. He created the poster *Waikiki Surf Festival*. Before you read, look carefully at the poster on your right. Make predictions about the artist.

1. What kind of life do you think he has?

2. What kind of hobbies do you think he has?

3. How do you think he gets ideas for his posters?

4. How do you think he became an artist? Do you think he studied art in college?

5. How does he make his posters?

Waikiki Surf Festival by Michael Cassidy. 1996.

C. Reading about an Artist and His Art.   Read this passage about Michael Cassidy and his art. As you read, try to answer this question:

• What are some similarities between being a surfer and being a good poster artist?

Michael Cassidy

Michael Cassidy believes that poster art is the art of **reduction**—taking things away so that the image is simple and easy to understand. It must give its message clearly, quickly, and memorably. Cassidy has used this art of reduction in his own life: he's been a surfer since high school days and spends
5 his time painting, being with his family, and surfing. He loves to travel and has visited some of the most beautiful places in the world: Tahiti, Hawaii, Mexico, Costa Rica, and Panama. "Most people work their whole lives, dreaming about where they'd go if they won the lottery," he says. "I've had the good fortune to go to those places, and I still dream about them."

10 Cassidy studied art at Palomar College in San Marcos, California, and at California State College at Long Beach. But he says he learned the most about his art by working in a sign shop. He has also learned a great deal by studying the masters of poster art: French poster artists from the beginning of the 20th century and American artists from the art deco period (the 1930s).

15 Cassidy's posters begin as paintings. He works on a **large scale**—his canvases can be seven feet high. He starts with a charcoal **sketch** (drawing), and then fills it in with oil paints. When he finishes, he photographs the painting, scans it into a computer, and then prints it using an ink jet printer.

It's not a coincidence that Cassidy has been a surfer all of his life. Surfing is a
20 sport of balance and **proportion**. In other words, the surfer must consider the size and shape of the board, the wave, and him- or herself in order to be successful. Cassidy uses these concepts in his art. In *Waikiki Surf Festival*, for example, Cassidy uses only a few simple **elements** (things or parts) to send the message: the waves, the sky, Diamond Head in the background, and in the front, the single figure,
25 balanced and confident.

Source: Margaret Moore, "Michael Cassidy" adapted and excerpted from *Hemispheres Magazine* (November 1997). Copyright © 1997. Reprinted by permission.

D. Discussion. Group Discuss the answers to these questions.

1. Check your predictions in Exercise B. Were you correct?

2. How is being a surfer like being a good poster artist?

3. Do you like Cassidy's art? Why or why not?

4. What other poster artists and poster art do you like? Are they examples of good poster art, according to Cassidy's philosophy?

E. Response Writing.   Choose *one* of these topics. Write about it for ten minutes. Don't worry about grammar and don't use a dictionary. Just put as many ideas as you can on paper.

- Describe your favorite kind of art. Choose *one* of the types you discussed in Exercise A or another one.
- Describe one of your favorite works of art: a painting, a sculpture, a photograph, or any other kind of work. Give the title and the artist if you know them. Say why you like it.
- Write about an artist. Explain how this artist's life is similar to or different from his or her art.
- Describe a poster that you like. Explain whether it follows Cassidy's ideas about poster art.

Part Two Everyday English: You Call That Art?

Before Listening

A. Thinking Ahead. **Group**   You are going to listen to Brandon and Chrissy talk about art. They discuss art that was popular in the 1960s and 1970s. Before you listen, look at these examples of art from the sixties and seventies.

Untitled by Donald Judd, 1967. An example of minimalist art

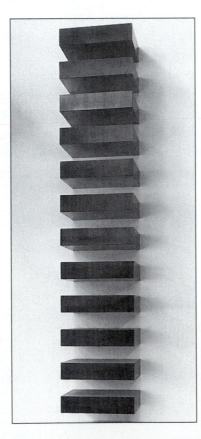

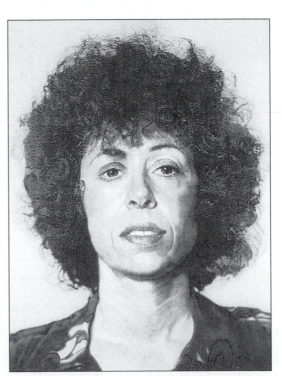

Linda by Chuck Close, 1975–76. An example of photorealism

100 Campbell Soup Cans by Andy Warhol, 1962. An example of pop art

Discuss the answers to these questions.

1. What do you see in each picture?

2. How does each picture make you feel?

3. Do you think any of these works has a message?

4. What do you think the artists were trying to say in each work?

5. Do you know anything about the style or artist of each picture?

B. Guessing Meaning from Context.

In the conversation in this part, the students use some words that may be new to you. The words are underlined in the sentences. Look for clues to their meaning in the words around them.

Write your guess in the blank after each sentence. Then check your guess with your teacher or the dictionary.

1. Tony Smith's steel cube is an example of <u>minimalist art</u> because it has a simple shape and it is made of only one material, steel.

Guess: _____

2. I like the art <u>movements</u> of the sixties and seventies—pop art, realism, minimalism—because they gave a truthful message about life.

Guess: _____

3. Minimalist art often uses <u>geometric shapes</u> such as cubes, circles, and boxes.

Guess: _____

4. Tony Smith's *Die* is in the <u>form</u> of a cube.

Guess: _____

5. Just <u>focus on</u> the shape of the cube. Don't think about the cube's message because it doesn't have one.

Guess: _____

6. The example of <u>photorealism</u> was so realistic that I thought it was a photograph, not a painting.

Guess: _____

7. Art often <u>reflects</u> the culture and society of the people who create it because it shows what people think is important at the time.

Guess: _____

C. Vocabulary Preparation: Informal Language.   In the conversation, the students use some informal words and expressions that may be new to you. First, read each sentence and guess the meaning of the underlined words. Then choose their meaning from the definitions in the box. Write the letter in the blanks.

Sentences

_____ **1.** Do you mean that it *wasn't* a photograph? It was so real looking that <u>I could have sworn</u> that it was a photograph!

_____ **2.** Disco music was <u>big</u> in the 70s—they played it on the radio and in all the dance clubs.

_____ **3.** I don't like disco music! <u>Give me</u> rock 'n roll anytime!

_____ **4.** Did you see the woman's face in the picture called *Linda*? You can see every line and spot <u>and all</u>!

_____ **5.** <u>Yuck</u>! I hate realistic art! I'd rather look at a piece of steel.

Definitions

a. and many things like that

b. I prefer

c. I was certain

d. That's disgusting!

e. popular

Listening

A. Listening for the Main Idea. [Video/Audio] Now listen
to the conversation. As you listen, try to answer this question:

• Why was realism a popular art movement in the sixties, according to Brandon?

B. Listening for an Explanation. [Video/Audio] Now listen
again. This time you are going to hear only part of the conversation. Listen to Brandon explain an art concept. Then answer this question.

• What do you think "art for art's sake" means?

_____

_____

C. Listening for Details. [Video/Audio] Listen again to part of the conversation. Listen for the
answers to these questions.

1. Do artists still create minimalist art today?

_____

2. What kind of art does Brandon call Andy Warhol's soup can work of art?

_____

3. What kind of art was the painting of the woman with hair on her leg, according to Brandon?

_____

After Listening

A. Vocabulary: Talking about Art. [Pair] When you talk about art, it's important to describe what
you see accurately. You are going to practice describing works of art. Before you do it, review some terms for describing art.

When you talk about a work of art, you usually describe the objects or people in the picture. Here are some other things you can say about a picture:

• Other things you see, such as shapes and colors in the picture
• The style of the painting, such as *minimalism* or *realism*
• Art processes: things the artist thought about or did as he or she created the work of art
• How the picture makes you feel

academic **Strategy**

Using Technical Terms

Each academic subject has its own set of special words. These words may only have meaning in that academic subject. These are called technical terms. For example, some technical terms for art are

- *minimalism*
- *proportion*

When you learn new technical terms for a subject you are studying, it's a good idea to use them in speaking or writing as soon as possible. This will help you understand them and remember them better.

Practice.   You have already learned some of the words in the following chart. Complete the chart with more words for each category. To do this, look at the picture on page 74 titled *Linda*. Discuss it with your partner. As you talk, add words that you use to the chart.

Shapes	Feelings	Art Styles	Art Processes
form	_____	minimalist	proportion
geometric	_____	realism	reduction
_____	_____	photorealism	reduce
_____	_____	_____	element(s)
_____	_____	_____	balance

B. Talking about Art.   **Pair**   Student A will describe one of the works of art on pages 79–81. Use the vocabulary from the chart above and answer these questions.

- What do you see in the picture?
- How does it make you feel?
- What do you think the artist was trying to communicate with this piece?

Student B will look at the same works of art and guess the title and artist of the work that Student A describes. Then switch roles.

speaking **Strategy**

Trusting Your Instincts

When you talk about art, you don't just describe it. It's also important to **interpret** it—describe what isn't actually in the picture, but what the picture or its elements suggest. Don't be afraid to interpret art. Rita Gilbert, a professional writer who specializes in art, tells students: "Trust your instincts. You know more than you think you know." She says that because we have lived with art all of our lives, we already have a lot of information about it.

Step One

Describe *one* of these works of art to your partner. First observe the work of art for a few moments. Then study the artist's techniques. What shapes, art style, and art process did the artist use? As you study the work of art, take a few notes and then describe it. (Note: The second picture on page 80 is a sculpture; the rest are paintings.)

Pergusa by Frank Stella, 1981.

Three Flags by
Jasper Johns,
1958.

*Blue Girl on Park
Bench* by George
Segal, 1980.

Self-Portrait with Model by Duane Hanson, 1979.

Step Two

Listen to your partner's description. Which of the works of art is your partner describing?

Part Three The Mechanics of Listening and Speaking

Language Function

Asking for Clarification: General

Sometimes in a conversation you don't understand a term or expression that the other person uses. If it's new to you, you may not even be able to repeat it. When this happens, you can ask for clarification with a general question. Here is an example:

A: Well, that's what you call minimalist art.

B: What?   **Less Formal**

B: I didn't get that.

B: What did you say?

B: Sorry, I didn't get that.

B: I didn't understand that.

B: Would you mind repeating that?

B: I'm sorry, what did you say?

B: Excuse me, I didn't understand that.   **More Formal**

A. Practice. **Audio**   Practice asking for general clarification. Listen to Student A's statements about art. Ask for clarification using one of the expressions in the box.

> **Expressions**
>
> What?   I didn't get that.
>
> What did you say?   Excuse me, I didn't understand that.
>
> Sorry, I didn't get that.   I'm sorry, what did you say?
>
> I didn't understand that.   Would you mind repeating that?

Example: A: Well, that's what you call minimalist art.

B: What did you say?

1. B: _____

2. B: _____

3. B: _____

4. B: _____

5. B: _____

6. B: _____

Language Function

Asking for Clarification: Specific   Audio

Once you know *what* you didn't understand, you need to ask for more specific clarification.

Here's the conversation that came before:

A: Well, that's what you call minimalist art.

B: What?

A: Minimalist art.

To get more specific clarification, now B can ask the following:

- What's that? OR: What is (minimalist art)?
- What does that mean?
- What kind of (art)? OR: What kind of (art) is that?
- Can you give me an example of (minimalist art)?

B. Practice.   Audio   Now practice asking more specific questions to get clarification. Listen to the same statements that you heard in Exercise A. First ask "What?" Then, when the speaker answers, ask for more specific information using one of these expressions:

- What's that? OR: What is _____?
- What does that mean?
- What kind of _____ is that?

Example: A: Well, that's what you call minimalist art.

B: What?

A: Minimalist art.

B: What's that?

1. B: _____

2. B: _____

3. B: _____

4. B: _____

5. B: _____

6. B: _____

Language Function

Giving Clarification [Audio]

When people ask you for general clarification, you don't always know exactly what they didn't understand. Sometimes you have to guess. To guess, you can repeat part of what you said. Here is an example:

A: Well, that's what you call minimalist art.

B: What?

A: <u>Minimalist</u>.

Then, when they ask for more specific information, you give it. Here is an example:

A: Well that's what you call minimalist art.

B: What?

A: Minimalist.

B: What does that mean?

A: <u>Well, that's a movement that had to do with reducing things to simple elements</u>.

Sometimes you know right away what the other person didn't understand. In that case, offer clarification immediately. Here is an example:

A: Well, that's what you call minimalist art.

B: What did you call it?

A: <u>Minimalist art. It means reducing things to simple elements</u>.

OR:

A: Well that's what you call minimalist art.

B: What kind of art?

A: <u>Minimalist. It means reducing things to simple elements</u>.

Notice that Speaker A gives clarification by defining a term. Speaker A can also clarify by giving an example:

A: <u>Minimalist art. You know, like the steel cube we saw today</u>.

C. Practice. **Audio** Listen to the following short conversations. For each conversation, decide if Speaker B is asking for general clarification or for more specific clarification. Check (✔) the type of question that you hear.

Examples: A: My favorite kind of art is pop art.

 B: What did you say? (General)

 OR:

 A: My favorite kind of art is pop art.

 B: Can you give me an example of that? (Specific)

	General	**Specific**
1.	☐	☐
2.	☐	☐
3.	☐	☐
4.	☐	☐
5.	☐	☐
6.	☐	☐

Intonation

Wh- Questions **Audio**

As you saw in Chapter Two, your voice goes up at the end of a *yes/no* question. When you ask a question with a *wh-* word (*who, what, when, where, why,* and *how*), your voice goes down at the end of the sentence. Listen to and study these examples:

• What kind of art is that?

• Who painted that?

• Where did you see that?

• When did you visit the museum?

Compare the intonation of *yes/no* questions to that of *wh-* questions:

• Is that an example of minimalist art?

• What is minimalist art?

D. Practice. (Audio)   Listen to each question. Is it a *yes/no* question or a *wh-* question? Check (✓) the type of question that you hear.

	Yes/No Question	Wh- Question
1.	☐	☐
2.	☐	☐
3.	☐	☐
4.	☐	☐
5.	☐	☐
6.	☐	☐

E. Practice. (Pair)   Have a conversation about art with your partner. Ask *wh-* questions. Discuss your opinions about art, artists, and art movements. Pay attention to question intonation as you speak.

Example: A: What kind of art do you like?

B: I like modern art.

A: Who's your favorite artist?

B: Andy Warhol.

Pronunciation

/I/ vs. /i/ (Audio)

Some learners of English have problems with the sounds /I/ and /i/. They may not hear the difference between the two sounds, or they may not be able to pronounce the two sounds correctly.
Here is an example of the difference in the two sounds:

/I/	/i/
Is that cube st<u>i</u>ll here?	I don't like that st<u>ee</u>l cube.

Here are more examples:

/I/	/i/
<u>i</u>t	<u>ea</u>t
sh<u>i</u>p	sh<u>ee</u>p
h<u>i</u>s	h<u>e</u>'s

Notice the different spellings for the /i/ sound. These are the most common spellings for this sound.

F. Practice. Audio   Listen to the following sentences. Circle the word that you hear.

1. It's a little bit / beet.

2. The bins / beans are over there.

3. Don't pick / peek at it.

4. She's still living / leaving.

5. The mitt / meat is here.

6. I see the ship / sheep in the picture.

G. Practice. Pair   Say one of the words in the box. (Don't say the words in order.) Your partner will write the word. Check the spelling of each word to see if it matches. If you didn't say it correctly, try again. Then exchange roles.

Word List			
sit	mitt	deep	meat
seat	bit	bean	beet
pick	his	he's	peek
bin	it	eat	live
leave	dip	sick	seek

H. Practice. Class   Now use words with these sounds in conversations. Interview your classmates. Use the following questions or use the Word List above to make up your own.

Find someone who

• likes <u>minimalist</u> art

• has ever <u>seen</u> Warhol's soup cans

• <u>lives</u> near a museum

• would like to <u>meet</u> a famous artist

• likes the painting *Three Flags* on page 80

• knows what was b<u>ig</u> in the sevent<u>ies</u> (Notice another spelling for the /i/ sound.)

• knows what was popular in the s<u>ix</u>t<u>ies</u> (Be careful! This word has both sounds.)

Review: Language Functions

Asking for Clarification and Giving Clarification **Video/Audio**

Listen to these examples of how to ask for and offer clarification. You'll use these functions in the next section.

Put It Together

Asking for and Giving Clarification

Student A chooses a topic from the following list and makes a statement about it. Student B asks for clarification. It can be general or specific, depending on how much Speaker B already knows. Student A offers clarification. If Student B asks a specific question, Student A offers a definition or an example. Remember to use correct question intonation. Pay attention to the /I/ and /i/ sounds. Take turns playing the roles of Student A and Student B.

Example: A: My favorite artist is Andy Warhol.

B: I'm sorry. I didn't get that.

A: Andy Warhol.

B: Who was he?

A: He painted *100 Campbell's Soup Cans.*

Topics

- my favorite artist
- my favorite kind of art
- my favorite work of art
- an art exhibit I saw recently
- something interesting I've learned so far in this chapter
- a famous artist from my culture or country
- the strangest, ugliest, or worst work of art I've ever seen

.:::⋮⋮ **Part Four** Broadcast English: The Art of George Segal

Before Listening

Becca by Henry Moore, 1965.

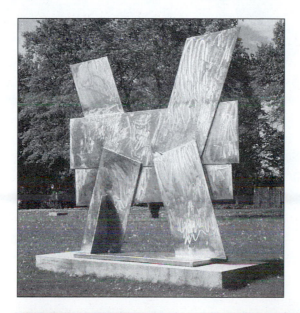

City on the High Mountain by Louise Nevelson, 1983.

Puppy by Jeff Koons, 1992.

A. Thinking Ahead. **Group**   You are going to hear a radio program about another artist. This artist, George Segal, is a modern sculptor. Talk about sculpture and sculptors. Discuss the answers to these questions.

1. What are some typical **subjects** of sculpture (the people or things shown in sculpture)?

2. In what kinds of places can you see sculpture?

3. How do sculptors make their works of art? What kinds of materials (steel, stone, clay, etc.) do they use?

4. What are the differences among the sculptures in the photos on this page and on page 89?

5. How is a sculpture different from a painting or a photograph?

6. What other famous sculptors or sculptures do you know?

B. Predicting. **Pair**   Before you listen, make a prediction about what you are going to hear. Look at the photo of one of George Segal's sculptures on page 80. Discuss the answer to this question.

• How do you think Segal makes his sculptures? (What kind of material does he use?)

C. Guessing Meaning from Context.
Before you listen to the radio program, guess the meaning of some words from the program. The words are underlined in the sentences. Look for clues to their meaning in the words around them.

Write your guess in the blank after each sentence. Then check your guess with your teacher or the dictionary.

1. The subjects of George Segal's work are very <u>mundane</u>—he shows ordinary people in the everyday moments of life.

   Guess: _____

2. However, Segal doesn't think ordinary life is <u>banal</u>. On the contrary, he thinks the everyday moments of life can be very interesting and special.

   Guess: _____

3. Segal's sculptures often look like <u>ghosts</u>. They are done in white plaster and you see these humanlike forms in art museums throughout the world.

   Guess: _____

4. The professor wasn't prepared to talk to the class, but she gave a very good <u>impromptu</u> lecture without any notes.

   Guess: _____

5. Edward Hopper shows the <u>bleakness</u> of city life in his paintings of cold, empty city streets.

   Guess: _____

6. The museum is having a <u>retrospective</u> exhibit of Andy Warhol's work. It's including examples of all of his work, from the beginning of his career until his death.

   Guess: _____

7. A <u>landscape</u> isn't always a country scene; you can also paint a city landscape, as long as it shows a wide view of a scene.

   Guess: _____

8. Segal's sculptures are the opposite of <u>abstract</u> art: He shows things in a realistic, or natural, way.

   Guess: _____

9. Segal placed his sculpture *Next Departure* in a lifelike <u>tableau</u>: Three people are in line to buy a ticket at a bus station.

   Guess: _____

D. Vocabulary Preparation: Idioms and Phrasal Verbs.
You will hear some expressions in the radio program: idioms and phrasal verbs. How many of them do you know? First, read each sentence and guess the meaning of the underlined words. Then choose their meaning from the definitions in the box. Write the letter in the blanks.

Sentences

_____ **1.** I <u>dropped by</u> my professor's office after class to ask her a question.

_____ **2.** When I paint, I am <u>dealing with</u> my emotions. My pictures show how I feel.

_____ **3.** He's not really happy, he's just <u>putting on an act</u>. He's actually a very unhappy person.

_____ **4.** We wanted to interview the artist, so we <u>caught up with</u> him at his studio.

_____ **5.** The artist tried to show the many ordinary moments that <u>make up</u> our lives.

<table>
<tr><td colspan="2">Definitions</td></tr>
<tr><td>a.</td><td>met with</td></tr>
<tr><td>b.</td><td>visited</td></tr>
<tr><td>c.</td><td>pretending</td></tr>
<tr><td>d.</td><td>fit together to form</td></tr>
<tr><td>e.</td><td>concerned with</td></tr>
</table>

academic Strategy

Using Your Culture Informant (Review)

There are some cultural references in the radio program. Do you know them?

- In one of Segal's works, a white figure sits on a real stool at a real <u>formica diner counter</u>.

- In another work, a man stands in a bar, under a <u>neon Budweiser sign</u>.

Practice.   If you don't know what these terms refer to, ask your informant what they mean.

Listening

Bust on a **pedestal** in the History Room at the Castello Del Miramare in Trieste, Italy.

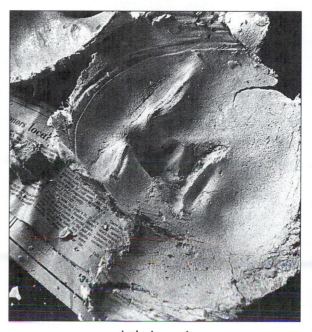

A **plaster cast**

A. Listening for the Main Idea. Audio Listen to the radio program. As you listen, try to answer this question:

- What are the subjects of Segal's sculptures?

listening **Strategy**

Using Similes to Guess Meaning Audio

When people talk about art, they use descriptive language. One kind of descriptive language is the use of **similes**. A simile is an expression that makes a comparison between two things. A simile can help you guess the meaning of a new word in a sentence. These expressions usually include <u>like</u>. Here is an example:

His sculptures were gargantuan, <u>like</u> giants with their heads in the sky.

If you know what giants are (very big people), you can guess that "gargantuan" means "very big."

B. Using a Simile to Guess Meaning. (Audio) Listen to a short excerpt from the radio program. It contains a simile. Use the simile to guess the meaning of this underlined word: a <u>haunting</u> life-sized human figure.

<u>Haunting</u> probably means _____

_____

C. Listening for Details. (Audio) Listen again to part of the program and answer these questions.

1. How did Segal first get the idea to use plaster bandages in his work?

_____

_____

2. When did Segal first get the idea to use plaster bandages in his work?

_____

_____

3. Why was Segal interested in using the plaster bandages in his work?

_____

_____

D. Analyzing Information. (Audio) Listen to another part of the program and answer this question.

• How is Segal's art different from abstract art?

_____

_____

_____

_____

listening Strategy

Listening for Impressions or Opinions   Audio

When people express their **impressions** (ideas) or opinions about something, they often use certain words and expressions to introduce them. When you hear these words and expressions, you know an opinion or impression is coming. Here are some examples:

- I think
- I feel
- I get a sense

E. Analyzing People's Impressions.   Audio   The interviewer has one idea of Segal's work. Segal has a different idea. Listen to this part of the radio program and try to answer this question. If necessary, listen to this part of the program again.

- How are the interviewer's impressions of Segal's work different from Segal's impression?

After Listening

A. Comprehension Check.   Pair   Discuss the answers to these questions.

1. What are the subjects of Segal's sculptures?

2. How does Segal make his sculptures? Explain the process in your own words.

3. How does Segal describe his own work? In other words, what does he say that he is showing us about life?

B. Discussion.   Group   Discuss the answers to these questions.

1. What is your opinion of Segal's work, based on the example you see on page 80?

2. Have you ever created any sculpture? If so, tell the group about the experience. If not, would you like to do a sculpture?

C. Thinking Creatively.   Group   Segal found an artistic use for something that was not intended for art—medical bandages. In your groups, think of a way to use non-art materials in art. You might start by brainstorming for everyday objects, and then think of how you can use them in art. Describe the material(s) and the process. When you finish, report your ideas to the rest of the class.

Example: Material: rubber bands

Artistic use: glue hundreds of them to a board and then spray paint them with different colors

..::::: **Part Five** Academic English: Pop Art

Before Listening

A. Brainstorming. (Group)   You are going to listen to a lecture about pop art. Pop art was an art movement of the 1960s. Pop artists used images from popular culture in their art: advertisements, comic books, and product packages. You have already seen an example of pop art: Andy Warhol's *100 Campbell Soup Cans* on page 75. In your group, think about the purpose of pop art. Discuss the answers to these questions.

1. Why do you think pop artists used these images?

2. What do you think these artists were trying to say in their art? For example, what does a picture of a soup can say?

Write your ideas down, and then share them with the class.

B. Thinking Ahead. (Group)   Look at the art on pages 100–105. The speaker will discuss these works in the lecture. Before you listen, think about how the lecturer might use these pictures in the lecture. Look at each one and discuss the answers to these questions.

1. What is the style of each picture?

2. What do you think each artist is trying to express?

3. What are the similarities among the pictures? What are the differences?

C. Guessing Meaning from Context.   In the lecture, you are going to hear some words that may be new to you. Before you listen, guess the meaning of some words from the lecture. The words are underlined in the sentences. Look for clues to their meaning in the words around them.

   Write your guess in the blank after each sentence. Then check your guess with your teacher or the dictionary.

1. Jackson Pollock's art shows us his <u>internal struggles</u>—the painful or confused feelings he had as he painted.

   Guess: _____

2. Like Pollock, some artists use art to express their <u>state of being</u>: You can see how they feel by looking at their work.

   Guess: _____

3. Billboards create <u>intense visual stimulation</u>—their bright colors and interesting images make it difficult for drivers to pay attention to the road.

   Guess: _____

4. The <u>consumer culture</u> that we live in makes us want to spend money on new products, even if we don't need them.

   Guess: _____

5. That painting reflects a feeling of <u>randomness</u> because the objects in it are not organized in any particular way.

   Guess: _____

6. The objects in the painting *Canyon* are not <u>unified</u>. Rather, they are mixed together with no connection to each other.

   Guess: _____

7. Pop art was <u>innovative</u> in that it used images in a new way.

   Guess: _____

8. Andy Warhol started as a <u>commercial illustrator</u>. He drew pictures for advertisements in magazines and newspapers.

   Guess: _____

9. Warhol liked the <u>streamlined</u> designs in advertising art, so he borrowed those simple styles to use in his own work.

   Guess: _____

10. Warhol didn't care about his subjects: He was equally <u>detached</u> from both soup cans and famous people.

    Guess: _____

11. Robert Rauschenberg is famous for using <u>found objects</u> in his paintings—old magazines, empty cigarette cartons, and other things he found while taking walks around New York City.

    Guess: _____

Listening

A. Listening for the Main Idea. **Audio** Listen to the lecture one time. Don't take notes. Don't worry about understanding everything. Just listen for the main idea. As you listen, try to answer this question:

- Who were two important pop artists?

listening **Strategy**

Viewing Images as You Listen **Audio**

Professors of <u>certain</u> subjects often use slides during their lectures. This is especially true in art history. (You might also see slides in subjects such as anthropology and biology.) It's important to pay close attention to the slide as you listen, but don't forget to continue taking notes. Write down the information about the image as the lecturer gives it to you. In some cases, it helps to sketch the image in your notes.

B. Listening for Information about an Image. **Audio** Listen to a part of the lecture. Look at the picture on page 100. As you listen, answer these questions.

1. Who is the artist? _____

2. What is the name of the painting? _____

3. Look for the "overlapping lines that swirl" that the lecturer describes. Draw a sketch of them here:

listening Strategy

Using Examples to Understand New Terms   **Audio**

Professors often give examples of new terms in their lectures. This helps you understand the terms. Sometimes examples follow the new term after the expression "such as." Here is an example:

The artist's work reflects a range of <u>sentiments</u>, such as <u>anger, confusion, and fear</u>.

(Examples follow the new word <u>sentiments</u>.)

Other clues for examples are these:

- For example, . . .
- One example is . . .
- Examples include . . .

C. Listening for the Meaning of New Terms.   **Audio**   Listen to these words in sentences from the lecture. The lecturer helps you understand them by giving examples. Write the examples that you hear. You'll hear the sentences two times.

1. mass-produced visual media = _____

   _____

2. heroic = _____

   _____

D. Taking Notes.   **Audio**   Listen to the lecture again. You will hear it in four parts. As you listen to each part, take notes using the outline on pages 100–105. Listen to each part as many times as necessary in order to complete the outline for that part.

As you listen, look at the art that accompanies each part. Notice the use of key words in the outline instead of complete sentences. Practice completing the notes in this way.

Pop Art

Part One

I. Introduction

   A. Pop art began _____in late 1950s_____

   B. Pop artists inspired by _____

    _____

II. The Difference Between Pop Art and Abstract Expressionism

   A. Abstract expressionism: movement that _____

    _____

   B. Autumn Rhythm refers to _____

    _____

   C. Pollock believed _____

    _____

   D. Abstract expressionism reflected _____

    _____

III. American Culture in the 1960s

   A. Television: _____

   _____

   B. Pop artists different from 1940s and 1950s artists because _____

   _____

   _____

Now listen again. When you have completed this part of the outline, go to the next part.

Part Two

IV. Robert Rauschenberg

   A. Background

     1. Born: _____

     2. Moved to New York: _____

   B. His goals: direct art away from _____ and toward

   _____

   C. Materials

     1. Examples: _____

     2. His art reflected _____

D. *Canyon*

    1. Description and date: _____

    2. Reflected: _____

E. In 1960s, was fascinated by _____

_____

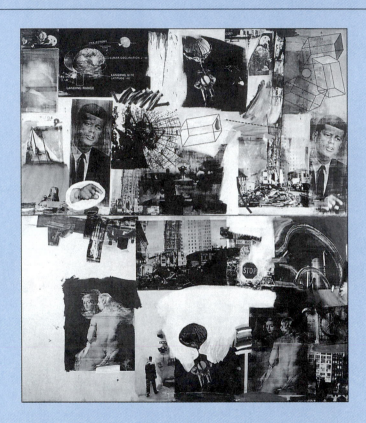

F. *Skyway*

    1. Description and date: _____

_____

    2. Gives viewer the sensation of _____

G. Rauschenberg's use of found objects was _____ and

_____

H. Pop artists were interested in _____ because

_____

Now listen again. When you have completed this part of the outline, go to the next part.

Part Three

V. Andy Warhol

  A. Background

    1. Born: _____

    2. Education: _____

    3. First job: _____

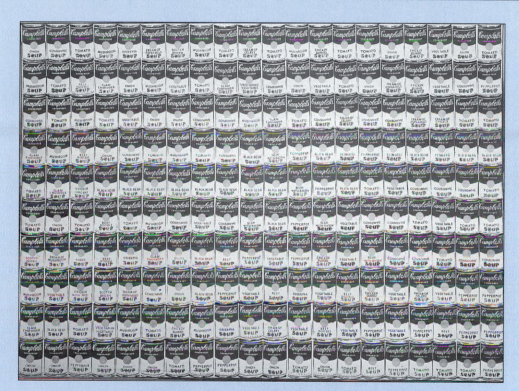

  B. Fine art painting: *200 Campbell's Soup Cans*

    1. Description and date: _____

    _____

    2. Showed his fascination for _____

    _____ and _____

    _____

C. Quote (Remember to use key words here!): _____

_____

_____

D. Ideas about fame: _____

_____

E. Warhol's portraits

1. Examples: _____

_____

2. Warhol wasn't interested in the people he painted; he was interested in

_____

F. Warhol's work reflects _____

_____

Now listen again. When you have completed this part of the outline, go to the next part.

Part Four

VI. Other Pop Artists

A. Other pop artists included Claes Oldenburg and Roy Lichtenstein

B. Oldenberg

   1. Sculptures look like _____ but they are

      _____

   2. Example: _____

C. Lichtenstein

   1. Was inspired by _____

   2. Example: _____

D. What pop artists saw: _____

Now listen again to this part of the outline.

After Listening

A. Using Your Notes. Pair   Use your notes to discuss the answers to these questions about the lecture.

1. What's the difference between abstract expressionism and pop art?

2. What was happening in American culture in the early 1960s? How did this influence pop art?

3. Who were two important pop artists? For each one, give one example of his or her work. Explain how it is an example of pop art.

4. Who were two other pop artists? Explain how their work is an example of pop art.

5. What other pop artists are you familiar with?

 speaking Strategy

Forming and Expressing an Opinion

It's important to have opinions and to express them in academic discussions. An opinion is more than a statement of like or dislike. You must also be prepared to support your opinion; in other words, say why you like or dislike something.

You can form your opinion while you listen to other people express theirs. Write notes while they express their opinions: Think about whether you agree or disagree, and how good their reasons are. You can also add or subtract ideas from what they say. Then use your notes when it is your turn to speak.

B. Expressing Your Opinion. Group   Tell the group your opinion of pop art. Do you like it? Why or why not?

Step **Beyond**

A. Giving a Presentation: Research. (Group)

You are going to give a short presentation to your group on a work of art. Select a work of art from the 1960s or 1970s. It can be a painting, a sculpture, a photograph, or a poster. You can use one in this book, or find one in an art book at the library.

You can also learn a lot about artists and their art at museums and galleries on the Web. One example is The Andy Warhol Museum site <www.warhol.org>. If possible, bring to class the art book or a copy of the painting (from the book or printed from a website) that you are going to discuss.

Note: Remember that website addresses change frequently.

B. Giving a Presentation: Planning.

Plan your presentation. Take notes. Use the following outline:

   I. Introduction

      A. Give the title of the work, the artist's name, and the date of the work.

      B. What movement does the work represent?

  II. Discussion of the Artist

      A. His or her background

      B. Other important works

 III. Description of the Artist's Work

      A. What do you see? (Who or what are the subjects?)

      B. How is it an example of the movement?

      C. What process(es) did the artist use to create this work?

      D. What is the purpose of the work? (What is the artist trying to express?)

Now give your presentation to your group. Use your notes. Remember to trust your instincts. After you listen to each others' presentations, ask questions to clarify information.

chapter Four

Ancient Greek Art

In this chapter, you'll listen to information about ancient Greek art. You'll also talk about myths and legends, and discuss how art informs us about ancient civilizations.

.·:·:·:· **Part One** Introduction: Ancient Greek Art and Civilization

Dipylon Vase

A. Thinking Ahead. **Pair** Talk about ancient Greece with your partner. Discuss the answers to these questions.

1. What do you know about ancient Greek civilization?

2. What do you know about Greek myths and legends?

3. What do you know about ancient Greek art?

B. Predicting. **Group** You are going to read about ancient Greek civilization and art. Before you read, look carefully at the picture of the *Dipylon Vase* above. Discuss the answer to this question.

• What might this vase tell us about ancient Greek culture?

C. Reading about Ancient Greek Civilization and Art.   Read the following passage about Greek civilization and art. As you read, try to answer this question:

• Why are Greek vases so important?

Greek Civilization and Art

No doubt a major reason that we respect the ancient Greeks is that they excelled in many different fields. Their political ideals serve as a model for contemporary democracy. Their poetry and drama and philosophy survive as living classics, familiar to every serious scholar. Their architecture
5 and sculpture have influenced most later periods in the history of Western art.

We assume that the Greeks' genius shone equally in painting, but we know very little about this because most painted works have been lost. We would know even less, except that a large number of painted clay vases were produced from about the 8th century B.C. These pots were made from **terra cotta** (baked
10 clay), an extremely strong material; it can break, but it won't disintegrate, and so the pieces can be reassembled. For this reason a large quantity of Greek art has survived to our day.

Not many cultures can match the Greeks in the elaborate painting of vases. These terra cotta vessels served as grave monuments, storage urns for wine or
15 oil, drinking cups, and so forth. An early example is the so-called *Dipylon Vase,* named for the cemetery in Athens where it was found. Made in the 8th century B.C., the *Dipylon Vase* offers a superb example of the geometric style of vase painting. This is the first clearly defined style we know the Greeks followed. The reason for the term "geometric style" is obvious. Much of the vase's deco-
20 rations consists of geometric lines and patterns, including the "meander" pattern that runs around the top just under the rim. Images of people are simply stick figures, and they are integrated wonderfully in the overall geometric design.

The *Dipylon Vase* offers us information on the burial customs of the Greeks,
25 especially as contrasted with the Egyptians. Objects found in the pharaoh Tutankhamun's tomb indicated he would enjoy a busy and prestigious afterlife, since that is what the Egyptians expected. The Greeks, on the other hand, were not so optimistic. To them, life after death was a gray and shadowy place, of little interest. A funerary urn like the *Dipylon Vase* was placed above the burial
30 spot to receive liquid offerings and was intended to show the respect of the deceased's relatives and friends. A funeral procession is painted on the vase. But there is no provision for enjoyment of the next world, only a recognition of the one left behind.

Source: Rita Gilbert, "Greek Civilization and Art" adapted and abridged from *Living with Art, Fourth Edition.* Copyright © 1995 by McGraw-Hill, Inc. Reprinted with the permission of the publishers.

D. Comprehension Check. Group Discuss the answers to these questions.

1. Why are Greek vases so important?

2. What were Greek vases made from? Why did they last so long?

3. Describe the painting style of the *Dipylon Vase.*

4. What does the *Dipylon Vase* tell us about ancient Greek civilization?

5. How were the ancient Greeks different from the ancient Egyptians?

E. Response Writing. Choose *one* of these topics. Write about it for ten minutes. Don't worry about grammar and don't use a dictionary. Just put as many ideas as you can on paper.

- Describe what you know or remember about ancient Greek civilization, Greek myths and legends, or ancient Greek art.

- Write about what you would like to know about ancient Greek civilization, Greek myths and legends, or ancient Greek art.

- Compare the *Dipylon Vase* to another work of art, from any time or civilization.

- Have you been to Greece? If so, describe your experience.

⠿ Part Two Everyday English: Greek Pottery

Before Listening

A. Thinking Ahead. Group You are
going to listen to Tanya and a teaching
assistant, Doug, talk about one type of
Greek art: pottery. Before you listen, look
at this photo of Greek pottery and discuss
the images on it in your groups.

As you did in Chapter Three, describe your impressions. Interpret what
you see. Remember to trust your instincts:
You know more than you think you know.
Who might the people be? Where do you
think the idea for the picture came from?

Interior of a *kylix,* a drinking cup. Around 490–480 B.C.

B. Guessing Meaning from Context.   Tanya and Doug use some words in their conversation that may be new to you. The words are underlined in the sentences. Look for clues to their meaning in the words around them.

Write your guess in the blank after each sentence. Then check your guess with your teacher or the dictionary.

1. Greek art <u>illustrates</u> many aspects of Greek civilization; for example, a Greek vase now in the Boston Museum of Fine Art shows a scene from one of the Greek myths.

   Guess: _____

2. The ancient Greeks showed their <u>ideals</u> in their art; for example, people represented in statues were always perfectly formed, strong-looking, and beautiful.

   Guess: _____

3. Instead of choosing an easy topic to write about, Tanya took the more <u>challenging</u> one.

   Guess: _____

4. Tanya found <u>source information</u> for her paper in an art book in the library. Both the photos of the pots and the text of the book gave her enough information to write her paper on ancient Greek pottery.

   Guess: _____

5. Greek pots survived because they were <u>durable</u>; they were made of a material that could last for a long time.

   Guess: _____

6. Greek pots are very <u>detailed</u>: You can see many small things in the scenes such as the weapons and tools that people used, their clothes, and even the way that they wore their hair.

   Guess: _____

C. Vocabulary Preparation: Idioms and Phrasal Verbs.   Tanya and Doug use some idioms and phrasal verbs in their conversation. How many of them do you know? First, read each sentence and guess the meaning of the underlined expressions. Then choose their meaning from the definitions in the box. Write the letter in the blanks.

Sentences

_____ **1.** You chose the most difficult assignment—<u>good for you</u>!

_____ **2.** We don't know much about that civilization because we don't have much to <u>go on</u>. The objects they created didn't survive.

_____ **3.** I'll <u>be out of here</u> by 5 P.M., so you can use my computer this evening.

_____ **4.** We have many Greek pots at the museum <u>dating from</u> the eighth century, B.C.

_____ **5.** Yes, <u>that will work</u>—I can meet you at 6 P.M.

Definitions

a. that's convenient

b. rely on; get information from

c. I'm proud of you; OR: You should be proud of yourself

d. that existed in

e. be leaving

Listening

A. Listening for the Main Idea.   **Video/Audio**   Now listen to the conversation. As you listen, try to answer this question:

• Why is Greek pottery so important in the study of ancient Greek culture?

B. Listening for Details. [Video/Audio]   Listen again to part of the conversation. Listen for information that answers these questions.

1. Why does Tanya need photos of pots?

_____

_____

2. Why did Greek pottery survive?

_____

_____

3. Where do we get information about ancient Greek civilization?

_____

_____

C. Listening for Inferences. [Video/Audio]   Now listen again. This time you are going to hear the first part of the conversation. Listen for the answer to this question.

• Why do you think Doug interrupts his phone call?

_____

_____

_____

D. Guessing Meaning from Context: Academic Life. [Video/Audio]   Tanya and Doug use some terms that describe academic life. Listen to parts of their conversation. Guess the meanings of these terms in context. Write your guesses in the blanks.

1. office hours = _____

_____

2. reading list = _____

_____

3. department secretary = _____

_____

After Listening

A. Information Gap. **Pair**   Work with a partner. One of you works on page 117. The other works on page 271. Don't look at your partner's page. You both will ask and answer questions and complete a chart.

Student A

It's a good idea to review Greek myths and legends when you study ancient Greek art. This is because ancient Greek art often **depicts** (shows) subjects from myths and legends. An important part of Greek mythology is the gods and goddesses. People who study art need to know their Greek and Roman names and the characteristics or activities that they represent. How much do you already know about them? (Refer to the vocabulary chart for help with difficult words.)

Ask your partner for the missing information and write the answers on your chart. Take turns asking and answering questions. Ask questions such as the following:

A: What is Aphrodite the goddess of?

B: Love and beauty.

B: What is Aphrodite's Roman name?

A: Venus.

Vocabulary

Terms	Meanings
prophecy	knowledge of future events
crafts	the art of making everyday objects that people use or wear, such as furniture and jewelry
commerce	business activities
the underworld	according to ancient Greeks' beliefs, the place where people went after death
fertility	the ability to have many children or to produce large crops
blacksmith	a person who makes things from metal, such as horseshoes

Major Greek Gods and Goddesses

Greek Names	Roman Names	Main Characteristics/Activities
Aphrodite	Venus	Goddess of __love and beauty__
Apollo	_____	God of archery, music, prophecy, light, medicine, and poetry
_____	Mars	God of war
Artemis	Diana	_____
Athena	_____	Goddess of crafts, wisdom, and warfare
Demeter	_____	Goddess of agriculture
Dionysus	Bacchus	_____
_____	Cupid	God of love
Hera	_____	Goddess of marriage; protector of women
Hephaestus	Vulcan	_____
_____	Mercury	God of commerce; the gods' messenger
_____	Pluto	God of the underworld

B. Discussion. Group   Discuss the answers to these questions.

1. What myths and legends do you know about the Greek gods and goddesses? Share them with your group.

2. What myths and legends do you know from other ancient cultures or civilizations? Share them with your group.

3. Are there any similarities between the myths and legends of one culture and another? What are they?

4. Why might it be important to know about ancient myths and legends?

5. Can you think of any works of art (from any time or place) that depict gods, goddesses, or stories from ancient myths and legends? If so, describe them to your group.

. . : : : : Part Three The Mechanics of Listening and Speaking

Language Function

Requesting an Explanation Audio

Sometimes in a conversation you have difficulty understanding more than just a word or expression; you don't understand an idea or a suggestion. When this happens, you ask for an explanation. Here are some ways to ask for an explanation:

Examples: A: What you need are very good photos of the pottery.

          B: Why?   **Less Formal**

             Well, what's the reason for that?

             Can you tell me why?

             Excuse me,* but why is that?

             Excuse me, but why do you say that?

             Excuse me, but would you mind explaining that?   **More Formal**

*Note:** Adding "excuse me" makes the request more polite.

A. Practice. **Audio**   Practice asking for an explanation. Listen to student A's statements. Ask for clarification using one of the expressions in the box.

Less Formal	More Formal
Why?	Excuse me, but why is that?
Well, what's the reason for that?	Excuse me, but why do you say that?
Can you tell me why?	Excuse me, but would you mind explaining that?

Example: A: You need good photos of Greek pottery.

B: Excuse me, but why is that?

1. B: _____

2. B: _____

3. B: _____

4. B: _____

5. B: _____

Intonation

Understanding Interjections **Audio**

Several interjections in English are common in informal conversation. They are very informal. Listen to this one from the conversation:

Doug: Well, what can I do for you?

Tanya: Uh, you know that paper that's due on Friday?

Here are some more examples.

Interjections	Meanings
• Uh-huh.*	Yes. OR:
	You're welcome.
• Uh-uh.*	No.
• Huh?	What? (Excuse me?)
• Uh . . . OR:	I'm thinking. OR:
Um . . .	I'm not sure what to say.
• Uh-oh!	I made a mistake. OR:
	There's a problem.

*Note: Uh-HUH (meaning "yes") is stressed on the second syllable. UH-uh (meaning "no") is stressed on the first syllable. This is an easy way to tell them apart.

B. Practice. **Audio**   Listen to each conversation. What does the second speaker mean? Check (✓) the answer.

Second Speaker's Meaning

Conversation	Yes	No	You're Welcome.	What?/ Excuse me?	There's a Problem!
1					
2					
3					
4					
5					

C. Practice. **Pair**   One of you plays the role of Student A, and the other is Student B. Follow the directions in the boxes.

Example: **Question:** Do you like Greek art?

   Answer: Uh-huh (Yes.)

Student A

Say the following to your partner. Wait for a response.

1. Have you ever been to Greece?   4. There's a large insect crawling on your shoe.
2. May I borrow your pencil?   5. Are you from Egypt?
3. Thanks a lot!

• Then respond to your partner's questions and responses. Use one of the interjections on page 119 in your response.

Student B

• Respond to your partner. Use one of the interjections on page 119 in your response.
• Then say each of the following to your partner. Wait for a response.

1. Do you speak Greek?   4. Could I borrow some money from you?
2. I think we're going to have a big test tomorrow!   5. Thank you.
3. Are you hungry yet?

Pronunciation

The *th* Sound* Audio

The letters *th* have two sounds in English. One of them is the sound in *th*anks. To pronounce the *th* sound, put the tip of your tongue *between* your teeth *just a little* and blow. *Don't stick your tongue between your lips!* If you don't put your tongue between your teeth, the *th* will sound like an /s/. Listen to these contrasts. Can you hear the difference?

s	th
<u>s</u>ing	<u>th</u>ing
<u>s</u>ink	<u>th</u>ink
<u>s</u>ank	<u>th</u>ank
ten<u>s</u>e	ten<u>th</u>
eight<u>s</u>	eigh<u>th</u>

Many ordinal numbers (which we use to refer to time periods in history) contain the *th* sound at the end. Here are some examples:

four<u>th</u> (4th)	seven<u>th</u> (7th)	ten<u>th</u> (10th)
fif<u>th</u> (5th)	eigh<u>th</u> (8th)	eleven<u>th</u> (11th)
six<u>th</u> (6th)	nin<u>th</u> (9th)	twelf<u>th</u> (12th)

Example: It's a Greek pot from the eighth century.

*Note: The IPA (International Phonetic Alphabet) symbol for this sound is /θ/.

D. Practice. Audio   In each pair of words, circle the one that you hear.

1. sank — thank

2. tense — tenth

3. sing — thing

4. sink — think

5. eights — eighth

6. some — thumb

7. sick — thick

8. seem — theme

9. sigh — thigh

10. saw — thaw

11. force — fourth

12. pass — path

E. Practice. Pair   Say one of the words on the list. (Don't say the words in order.) Your partner will write the word. Check each word to see if it matches. If your partner didn't write the correct word, try again. Then exchange roles.

Word List		
sank	tense	thing
tenth	thank	fourth
some	eights	sink
sigh	sing	think
force	thick	seem
thumb	eighth	theme
saw	thigh	pass
thaw	sick	path

F. Practice. Group   Now use words with the *th* sound in conversations. Interview your classmates. Use the following questions or use the words in the list in Exercise E above to make up your own. Write your classmates' names on a chart like the following. Which student collects the most names?

Find someone who . . .	Names
has something in his/her pocket	
is going to pass all his/her courses	
knows what happened in the eighth century, B.C. in Greece	
thinks Greek art is interesting	
likes to sing	
has been sick this year	
knows what day the tenth of this month is/was	

Review: Language Functions

Requesting an Explanation   Video/Audio

Listen to these examples of requesting an explanation. You'll use this function in the next section.

Put It Together

Requesting an Explanation   Pair

Student A chooses a topic from the following list and makes a statement about it. Student B requests an explanation. Then Student A gives an explanation. As you speak, use the interjections from the list on page 119 whenever appropriate. Pay attention to the *th* sound. Take turns playing the roles of Student A and Student B.

Example: A: I learned that most of the information that we have about ancient Greek civilization comes from pictures on pots.

              B: Excuse me, but why is that?

              A: Uh . . . because the pottery was durable.

              B: Thanks.

              A: Uh-huh.

Topics

- something interesting I learned so far in this chapter
- a famous myth or legend I remember from childhood
- my favorite Greek god or goddess
- a similarity between a Greek god, goddess, or myth and one from another culture
- what I like/dislike about art from ancient civilizations
- why it is/is not important to know about ancient myths and legends

. . : : : : Part Four Broadcast English: Ancient Greek Statues

Before Listening

A. Thinking Ahead. Group

You are going to hear a radio program about the sculpture of ancient Greece. Before you listen, review what you know about sculpture. Review part of the discussion you had about sculpture in Chapter Three: How do sculptors make their works of art? What kinds of materials do they use? Also, discuss the answer to this question.

• How do you think ancient Greek statues were made?

B. Guessing Meaning from Context.

Before you listen to the radio program, guess the meaning of some of the words from the program. The words are underlined in the sentences. Look for clues to their meaning in the words around them.

Write your guess in the blank after each sentence. Then check your guess with your teacher or the dictionary.

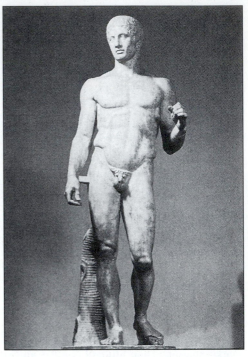

Roman copy of a Greek original. About 450–440 B.C.

1. Factories use <u>assembly lines</u> to produce many objects at once.

   Guess: _____

2. I thought my vase was a one-of-a-kind art object, but I discovered that it was <u>mass-produced</u>.

   Guess: _____

3. Most furniture manufacturers take <u>custom orders</u>. For example, you can ask for a certain kind of fabric to cover a chair.

   Guess: _____

4. After the earthquake, the terra cotta statues broke into a million pieces. The <u>fragments</u> were all over the museum floor.

   Guess: _____

5. Some archaeologists thought that the ancient Greeks were <u>cannibals</u> because it looked as though some people were eating body parts in a pot painting.

Guess: _____

C. Vocabulary Preparation: Synonyms.   Some of the words you will hear in the program have familiar synonyms. How many of them do you know? First, read each sentence and guess the meaning of the underlined words. Then choose their meaning from the definitions in the box. Write the letter in the blanks.

Definitions

a. clay; terra cotta   *d.* dug up

b. ancient times   *e.* took apart

c. naked

Sentences

_____ **1.** You can learn a lot about history by studying the art of <u>antiquity</u>.

_____ **2.** Archaeologists have <u>unearthed</u> many ancient Greek statues of gods and goddesses.

_____ **3.** They also have found several <u>earthenware</u> pots with detailed scenes painted on them.

_____ **4.** Ancient Greek statues of men were usually <u>nude</u>.

_____ **5.** The chef carefully <u>dismembered</u> the entire chicken before putting the body parts into boiling water.

D. Vocabulary Preparation: Technical Terms.   Here are some technical terms that you'll need to know before you listen to the radio program. Read the terms and their meanings. Ask the class if anyone has ever seen these items or examples of them.

Terms	Meanings
smelted (verb)	A process of melting an ore to separate out the metals that it contains. (In this context, "smelted" is used in a different way: Attaching metal pieces to each other to make statues. The sculptor sticks the pieces together using melted metal as a kind of glue.)
lost-wax casting (noun)	A method for making metal sculpture. A sculptor builds a mold around a wax object that duplicates the shape of the desired sculpture. Then the sculptor heats the mold and the wax melts. The sculptor then pours molten (melted) metal into the mold and it replaces the wax.
endoscope (noun)	A medical instrument that archaeologists use. It is a small camera attached to a tube. The tube can go into small or hard-to-reach places (such as the human body or a statue) and take pictures.

Listening

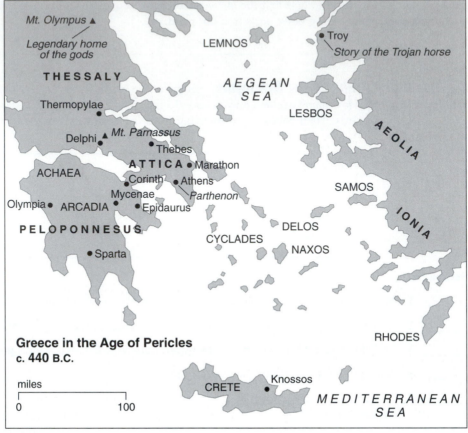

Greece in the Age of Pericles
c. 440 B.C.

miles
0   100

Ancient Greece. About 440 B.C.

A. Listening for the Main Idea. `Audio` Listen to the radio program about ancient Greek statues one time. As you listen, try to answer this question:

• What do we now know about how ancient Greek statues were made? How do we know this?

B. Listening for Details. `Audio` Listen to parts of the radio program and answer these questions.

1. Does the information about how Greek statues were made make them seem less valuable, in Carol Mattusch's opinion?

_____

_____

2. What did people in the 1800s think about the ancient Greeks when they first saw a pot painting showing the ancient statue workshops?

_____

_____

3. Why were there three different versions of a statue of Aphrodite, in Mattusch's opinion?

_____

_____

4. What does a beard indicate on a statue of a man from classical times?

_____

_____

academic Strategy

Understanding Time Abbreviations Audio

Archaeologists use certain time abbreviations to refer to the past. You might hear some or all of the following when people talk about the ancient world:

- Abbreviations for time periods before the Year 1 in the Western calendar include these:

  B.C.   =   Before Christ

  B.C.E. =   Before the Common Era

- Abbreviations for time periods from the Year 1 to the present include these:

  C.E.   =   Common Era

  A.D.   =   Anno Domini (Latin: Year of our Lord)

Note: Think of a timeline as a number line.

Practice.   Put these dates in order on the timeline before or after the Year 1:

440 B.C.   200 C.E.   500 A.D.   400 B.C.   600 B.C.E.

Year

_____ _____ _____   1   _____ _____

listening Strategy

Listening for Time Periods `Audio`

It's important to hear the centuries that a speaker refers to in a history lecture. As you saw in Part Three, we refer to centuries using ordinal numbers. Most of these end in the *th* sound. For example, make sure that you hear the difference between these two time periods:

the <u>first</u> century   the <u>fourth</u> century

It's also important to listen for the abbreviation that means a date is before or after the Year 1, as you saw in the Academic Strategy box on page 127. For example, make sure that you hear the difference between these two sets of time periods:

the fourth century B.C.   the fourth century A.D.

the eighth century B.C.E.   the eighth century C.E.

C. Listening for a Time Period. `Audio`   Listen to an excerpt from the radio program. Fill in the blanks with the correct time period information.

Well, in the _____ and the _____ centuries _____, in what we would call high classical times, the most popular type of statue was a naked male.

After Listening

A. Discussion. `Group`   Discuss the answers to these questions.

1. How did people in the past think Greek statues were made?

2. What do we now know about how ancient Greek statues were made? How do we know this?

3. Do you think the art historian Carol Mattusch was disappointed when she learned how Greek statues were actually made?

4. What mistaken belief did people in the 1800s have about ancient Greek civilization?

5. Can you think of any other misunderstandings that people have had about a foreign or ancient culture? How did they make the mistake? How did they correct it?

6. Have you ever seen a Greek statue? If so, tell where you saw it, what it looked like, and what you thought of it.

B. Using Art to Analyze a Civilization. **Group**   Archaeologists often study art objects, for example, pots and statues, to learn about ancient civilizations. You are going to do the same thing. Follow these steps:

Part One

1. Form two groups. One group is Civilization X. The other is Civilization Y.

2. Each group gets on opposite sides of the classroom.

3. In your groups, choose one or two kinds of art, for example, sculpture, pottery, or painting.

4. Now choose an important idea, activity, or kind of person that represents your culture. Here are some examples:

   ✓ Idea: In our culture, most people believe that there is life after death.

   ✓ Activity: Sports and games are important in our culture.

   ✓ Person: A leader in our culture, whether a man or a woman, wears a long dress.

5. Have an artistic member of your group draw the art object. Draw it so that it clearly shows the idea, activity, or person that you chose to represent your culture.

Part Two

1. Now you are a group of modern archaeologists. Exchange drawings.

2. In your group, guess what the other civilization's art object says about its culture.

 speaking **Strategy**

Correcting a Misunderstanding

In academic discussions, you often have to tell someone that he or she is mistaken. It's important to do this in a polite way. Starting the correction with an apology ("I'm sorry, but . . .") is the best way to do this. You can correct a misunderstanding formally or informally, depending on the situation.

Examples: Sorry. That's not right. It's a robe, not a dress.   **Less Formal**

I'm sorry, but you're mistaken. It's a robe, not a dress.

I'm sorry, but I think you're mistaken. It's a robe, not a dress.

I'm sorry, but I'm afraid you're mistaken. It's a robe, not a dress.   **More Formal**

3. Report your guesses to the other group. Correct any misunderstandings. Use the examples in the box as a guide.

4. Discuss the process of analyzing a civilization through its art. Is the process a good idea? Why or why not?

::::: **Part Five** Academic English: Ancient Greek Art

Before Listening

A. Predicting. **Group**   You are going to listen to a lecture about ancient Greek art. You have already seen and heard about two kinds of Greek art: pottery and statues. In the lecture, you will hear about an additional type of art. What other kind of art may have survived since ancient times? (Hint: It's something people wear.)

B. Thinking Ahead. **Group**   Look at the art on pages 134–139. The speaker will discuss these works of art in the lecture. Before you listen, think about how the lecturer might use these pictures. Discuss each one.

1. Figure 1: Do you recognize this building? Where is it?

2. Figure 2: Why do you think this statue is nude?

3. Figure 3: How is this statue different from Figure 2?

4. Figure 4: What can you see in the painting on this vase?

5. Figure 5: What can you see in the painting on this vase?

6. Figure 6: On what part of the body do you think ancient Greeks wore this object?

C. Guessing Meaning from Context.   In the lecture, you are going to hear some words that may be new to you. Before you listen, guess the meaning of some words from the lecture. The words are underlined in the sentences. Look for clues to their meaning in the words around them.

    Write your guess in the blank after each sentence. Then check your guess with your teacher or the dictionary.

Interior of a *kylix*, a drinking cup. Around 490–480 B.C.

1. Could you show me a <u>frontal</u> view of the statue? I've already seen the back.

   Guess: _____

2. The goddess Athena Parthenos was very important to the ancient Greeks. That's why they built the Parthenon and <u>dedicated</u> it to her.

   Guess: _____

3. The ancient Greeks had a lot of <u>admiration</u> for the human body. We can see this in the perfectly formed statues that they created.

   Guess: _____

4. You can see from that nude statue that the subject was an athlete: his <u>musculature</u> was very clearly carved by the sculptor.

   Guess: _____

5. Sorry, I can't think of an example of ancient Greek jewelry; nothing <u>comes to mind</u>.

   Guess: _____

6. A Greek vase called a *kylix,* or cup, is an example of a <u>utilitarian</u> art object. People used them every day in their homes.

   Guess: _____

7. We know that some people were buried with their jewelry because archaeologists have found it with them in their <u>tombs</u>.

   Guess: _____

D. Vocabulary Preparation: Technical Terms. Here are some technical terms that you'll need to know before you listen to the lecture. Read the terms and their meanings. Ask the class if anyone has ever seen these items or examples of them.

Terms	Meanings
glazing (noun)	A coating painted onto ceramic pots. It becomes glassy (hard and shiny, like glass) when it is heated.
kiln (noun)	An oven in which ceramic pots are heated. The heat makes them permanently hard.

Listening

A. Listening for the Main Idea.   Audio   Listen to the lecture one time. Don't take notes. Don't worry about understanding everything. Just listen for the main idea. As you listen, try to answer this question:

• What three kinds of Greek art does the speaker discuss in this lecture?

B. Listening for Meaning in Context.   Audio   Listen to parts of the lecture. You will hear the speaker give definitions of some terms. Listen for the meanings of the terms. Write the definitions that you hear using your own words in the blanks.

1. kouros = _____

_____

_____

2. kore = _____

_____

_____

3. contrapposto = _____

_____

_____

4. torques = _____

_____

_____

5. diadems = _____

_____

_____

listening Strategy

Using Phonetic Symbols to Write Foreign Words   Audio

You are going to hear several Greek names in this lecture. They may be foreign sounding and you may not know how to spell them when you hear them. You can write foreign-sounding names phonetically, that is, using letters or symbols that represent sounds. One system that can be used is the IPA (International Phonetic Alphabet). Here are some examples of words transcribed using IPA symbols from this chapter:

Greek Names

Parthenon	/'par θə nan/	Actaeon	/'æk te an/
Dipylon	/'di pə lan/	Olympia	/o 'lɪm pi ə/
Athena	/ə 'θi nə/	Pergamon	/'pɚ gə man/
kouros	/'ku ros/	Laocoon	/le 'o ko an/
Hephaestus	/hə 'fɛs təs/	Andokides	/æn 'do kə diz/
Delphi*	/'dɛl fi/	Artemis	/'ar tə mɪs/
kore	/'kɔr re/		

*Also (in English): /'dɛl fai/

C. Listening to Foreign-Sounding Names.   Audio   Listen to part of the lecture. Use phonetic symbols to write these names as you hear them.

1. Archaic = _____

2. Aphrodite = _____

3. Praxiteles = _____

4. Knidos = _____

D. Taking Notes.   Audio   Listen to the lecture again. You will hear it in four parts. As you listen to each part, take notes using the outline on pages 134–139. Listen to each part as many times as necessary in order to complete the outline for that part.

As you listen, look at the art that accompanies each part. Notice the use of key words in the outline instead of complete sentences. Practice completing the notes in this way.

Ancient Greek Art
——————
Part One

I. Introduction

FIGURE 1
The Parthenon

A. Parthenon as an example of ancient Greek art

   1. Built between _____

   2. Dedicated to _____

   3. Located on _____

B. Five periods in Greek art

   1. Classical—dates: _____

   2. Geometric—dates: _____

   3. Orientalizing—dates: _____

   4. Archaic—dates: _____

   5. Hellenistic—dates: _____

Now listen again. When you have completed this part of the outline, go to the next part.

Part Two

II. Greek Sculpture

  A. Basic Characteristics

    1. Three positions: _____

      _____

    2. Difference between female and male figures: _____

      _____

    3. Earliest _____ sculpted by Praxiteles for the city of Knidos, Asia Minor

FIGURE 2
Kouros

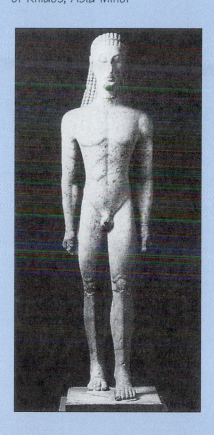

    4. Kouros is: _____

      _____

    5. Kore is: _____

      _____

B. Classical Period vs. Hellenistic Period

   1. Classical period

FIGURE 3
The Spear Bearer

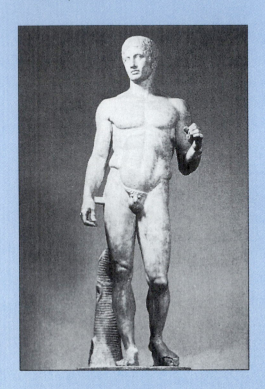

   a. *The Spear Bearer*: musculature becomes: _____

   _____

   b. *Contrapposto* is: _____

   _____

   2. Hellenistic period

   a. Figures show: _____

   b. Three examples of this: images of _____,

      sculpture from the city of _____,

      and *Laocoon and His Sons*, in the _____

Now listen again. When you have completed this part of the outline, go to the next part.

Part Three

III. Vase Painting

   A. Description

   1. Subject matter: _____

   2. Made by: _____

   3. Uses: _____

   B. Techniques

   1. Artists perfected different techniques of _____

   2. Purpose of glaze: _____

   _____

   3. Decorated with bands that _____

   _____

   C. Styles in different periods

FIGURE 4
Dipylon Vase

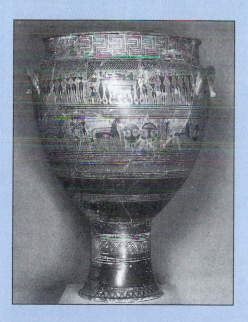

   1. Geometric period

   a. Vases have _____ designs

   b. Figures appear: _____

2. Archaic period

   a. Painters and potters start to: _____

   _____

   b. Popular technique of this period: _____

   _____

3. Later Andokides Painter developed _____

   _____ technique

Now listen again. When you have completed this part of the outline, go to the next part.

Part Four

IV. Jewelry

FIGURE 6

Diadem, late fourth century

    A. Who wore it: _____

    B. Type: _____

    C. Much didn't survive because: _____

                 _____

    D. Some jewelry has survived. Examples:

        1. _____

        2. _____

        3. _____

V. Conclusion

    A. Because of _____ Greek art exported throughout
       the Mediterranean

    B. Greek ideals were carried to the _____ and everywhere else

       that _____ went

Now listen again to this part of the outline.

listening **Strategy**

Using a Timeline to Take Notes Audio

There are different ways to take lecture notes. Some ways depend on your thinking style. Some depend on the topic of the lecture. Sometimes it is a good idea to use a timeline to take notes when you are listening to a history or art history lecture.

A timeline is a vertical or horizontal line with dates on it in chronological order (time order). Next to (or below) the dates you can write down names of the people, objects, or events associated with the dates. Look at this timeline of art movements in Europe from the 1700s to the present:

1750 .... 1800 .... 1875 .... 1900 2000

Neoclassicism   Romanticism   Impressionism   Expressionism   Neo-Expressionism

E. Using a Timeline. Audio   Listen to the first part of the lecture. Complete the following timeline with the time periods that you hear. (The lecturer didn't give the periods in chronological order, so building a timeline will help.)

Write the time periods in the blanks. Don't worry about the "Examples" column or the "Centuries" column for now; you'll fill them in later.

Examples	Time Periods (in chronological order)		Centuries
d	**Geometric** _____ 900 _____ – _____ 700 _____		_____ 8th _____ century B.C.E.
	Your own: _____ – _____		_____ century B.C.E.
	Orientalizing _____ – _____		_____ century B.C.E.
	Your own: _____ – _____		_____ century B.C.E.
	Archaic _____ – _____		_____ century B.C.E.
	Your own: _____ – _____		_____ century B.C.E.
	Classical _____ – _____		_____ century B.C.E.
	Your own: _____ – _____		_____ century B.C.E.
	Hellenistic _____ – _____		_____ century B.C.E.

F. Listening for Examples. **Audio** Now listen to part of the lecture. The lecturer will discuss examples of art that go with particular time periods. As you listen, put the letter of the art example in the column next to its time period in the timeline on page 140.

Art Examples

a. nude female figure

b. athletic musculature in statues

c. figures show more emotion

d. earliest vase with geometric designs: the *Dipylon Vase*

e. black figure technique in pottery becomes popular

f. standing male figure: *kouros*

---

 academic Strategy

Interpreting Time Periods **Audio**

Sometimes a speaker will refer to a time period precisely, for example, "between 480 and 320 B.C.E." Sometimes, however, a speaker may refer to a time period more generally, for example, "the third century." It's a good idea to be able to go back and forth from the specific to the general time periods when you are listening to a history lecture.

Practice. Work with a partner. Use the timeline on page 140. Use the periods in the timeline and make up your own. Say a specific time period to your partner. Your partner will then write the corresponding century into the "Centuries" column. Then switch roles.

Examples: A: [Says] 700 to 600 B.C.E.

B: [Writes] 7th century.

B: [Says] 550 to 600 B.C.E.

A: [Writes] 6th century.

After Listening

Using Your Notes. **Group** Use your notes to answer the following questions about the lecture.

1. What three kinds of Greek art does the speaker discuss in this lecture?

2. What does Greek sculpture tell us about the Greek feeling about the human body?

3. What were Greek vases used for?

4. What did the paintings on the earliest Greek pots look like?

5. What are the two main techniques of pot design?

6. What kind of jewelry did the ancient Greeks wear? Who wore it?

Step Beyond

A. Giving a Presentation: Research.   You are going to give a short presentation to your group on an example of ancient Greek art. Select one of the following:

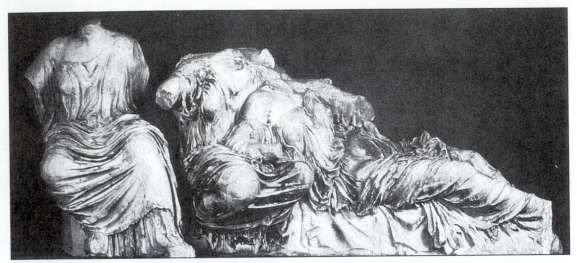

The Three Goddesses. About 438–432 B.C.

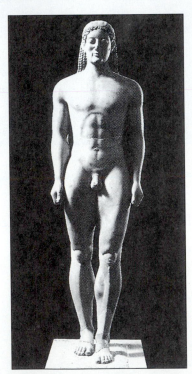

Kroisos. About 525 B.C.

Agesander, Athenodorus, and Polydorus of Rhodes.
Laocoon Group. Late second century, B.C.

You are going to present the work of art that you chose in the following way:

- describe it

- say what period it is from (Hellenistic, Classical, etc.)

- explain what it tells us about ancient Greek civilization

If you want to do research, you can find an art book at the library or visit an online museum. As you do research, use an outline like the one you saw in Chapter Three to take notes and to plan your presentation.

 speaking Strategy

Giving a Presentation from Notes

When you give a presentation, it's a good idea to speak from notes, not read an essay. One way to do this is to make a detailed outline of what you want to discuss. Read your outline many times—try to memorize it. Then make a less detailed outline, with just the main points (for example, the Roman numeral headings and the capital letter headings.) See if you can remember the missing details. Then make an outline with only the Roman headings. When you can give your presentation by just glancing at these headings, you're ready to speak in front of the class. This way, you can make eye contact and be a more interesting speaker.

B. Giving a Presentation: Presenting.
Now give your presentation to your group. Use your notes. Remember to make eye contact. After you listen to each others' presentations, ask questions to request further explanation.

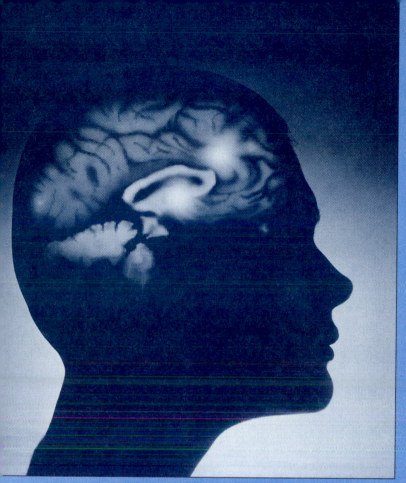

unit 3

Psychology

chapter
Five

States of Consciousness

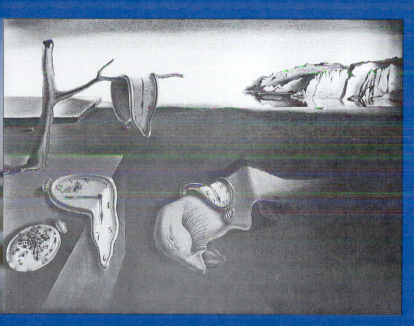

In this chapter, you'll listen to information about why we sleep and why we dream. You'll also discuss different theories about the process of sleep and dream interpretation.

Part One Introduction: What Do Your Dreams Mean?

A. Thinking Ahead. Group Discuss the answers to these questions about dreams.

1. What do you think dreams mean? What do you know about dream **interpretation** (analysis)? Share your ideas with the group.

2. Have you ever dreamed that you were flying? What do you think this kind of dream means?

3. If a person dreams about flying and in the dream has difficulty staying **aloft** (up in the air), what do you think that means? What does it mean if this person keeps bumping into things in her flying dream? What does it mean if she feels that she is flying to get away from danger?

B. Reading an Interpretation of a Dream. You are going to read a letter from the Ask the Dream Doctor website, where people describe dreams to the Dream Doctor and he interprets them. As you read, try to answer this question:

• What's the Dream Doctor's interpretation of Sheila's dream?

Sheila's Dream

Dear Dream Doctor,

Ever since I was about 7 years old, I have had the same dream. I am flying in the air, but I always have trouble staying up. I never touch the ground, but it is difficult for me to keep my arms flapping to stay up in the air. Sometimes I hit power lines
5 or just barely miss them. Usually when I am flying, it is to get away from someone! I am 25 years old now and I have had this dream maybe once or twice a week since the age of 7. Please help me understand this dream!

—Sheila, Age 25
Phoenix, AZ, USA

10 Hi Sheila,

Many people enjoy flying dreams. However, not all flying dreams are the same. Some are exhilarating and are accompanied by a sense of power and freedom—we fly easily and are thrilled by the view below us. In others, however, like yours, we have difficulty staying aloft and seem to be flying in order to escape danger.

15   Power lines are a **recurring** (repeating) symbol in flying dreams. Dreamers frequently write of "trying to fly above the power lines" or of bumping into them. I believe that *how* we are flying in our dreams—whether we are soaring easily or struggling to stay aloft—is an indication of our personal sense of power.

  Because flying dreams recur so frequently for you, I suggest that you try to
20 create the association in your mind that, whenever you are flying, you must be dreaming. The activity of flying can serve as a reminder that you must be dreaming, which will then allow you to explore your dreams consciously—this is also known as **lucid dreaming.**

  Your dream suggests that your life right now may be something of a "struggle
25 to stay aloft." Once you recognize that you are dreaming, why don't you ask yourself in the dream what the power lines that you keep bumping into represent? I would be interested to know your response in the dream to your question. In the meantime, what, or who, do you think the power lines symbolize? Whatever it is, I think it is a situation you want to get **on top of** (in control of).

Source: Charles McPhee, adapted and excerpted from "Ask the Dream Doctor." Available from www.dreamdoctor.com; INTERNET. Reprinted with the permission of Dr. Charles McPhee.

C. Discussion. `Group`   Discuss the answers to these questions.

1. Do you agree with the Dream Doctor's interpretation of Sheila's dream? Whether you do or not, how else would you explain dreams about flying—flying to escape danger, running into power lines, and having a difficult time staying aloft?

2. Do you ever have recurring dreams? If so, describe one. What do you think the dream means? Why do you think it recurs?

3. The Dream Doctor refers to lucid dreaming. Describe what you think this means in your own words. Have you ever had a lucid dream?

4. Do you think that dream interpretation (such as the Dream Doctor's) is useful? Do you think it can sometimes cause problems? Explain your answer.

D. Response Writing.   Choose *one* of these topics. Write about it for ten minutes. Don't worry about grammar and don't use a dictionary. Just put as many ideas as you can on paper.

- Do you think that dreams have meaning? What is the purpose of dreaming? Explain your answer.

- Describe an unusual or recurring dream that you have had. Explain what you think it means.

- What are the advantages and disadvantages of having a doctor interpret a person's dreams?

. : : : : : **Part Two** Everyday English: Do You Remember Your Dreams? (Interview)

Before Listening

A. Thinking Ahead. **Group**   You are going to listen to Chrissy interview people on the street. She's going to ask them if they remember their dreams. Before you listen, discuss the answers to these questions.

- Do you remember your dreams? If you don't, do you know why not?

B. Predicting. **Group**   You are going to listen to six people answer the question: "Do you remember your dreams?" What do you think most people will say? Do most people remember their dreams? In your groups, make predictions.

C. Vocabulary Preparation.   The students in the interview use some words and expressions that may be new to you. First, read each sentence and guess the meaning of the underlined word. Then choose their meaning from the definitions in the box. Write the letters in the blanks.

Sentences

_____ 1. Last night I dreamed that I ran in the Boston <u>marathon</u> and won! That's pretty strange, considering that, in the dream, I had a broken leg . . .

_____ 2. Even though I had a broken leg, I <u>managed</u> to win the race because I flapped my arms and flew over all the other runners.

_____ 3. I had a very funny dream last night. I think I had it because I went to sleep right after watching my favorite <u>sitcom</u> on TV.

_____ 4. I haven't seen my brother in years, but I had a dream about him last night. Then, <u>from out of the blue</u>, he called me today.

_____ 5. I dreamed that I found a hundred dollar bill on the street. When I reached down to pick it up, though, it <u>turned into</u> a snake and bit me.

Definitions

a. became

b. a long foot race

c. situation comedy: a type of TV program where people resolve a difficult situation in a funny way

d. was able to

e. without any advance notice

Listening

A. Listening for the Main Idea. (Video/Audio)   Now listen to the interview. As you listen, try to answer this question:

• Are most people willing to answer Chrissy's questions?

B. Listening for Details. (Video/Audio)   Now listen again. Which speakers remember their dreams? Circle *yes* or *no* in the chart.

  Then listen again. This time, listen for how often people remember their dreams: In other words, do they remember them all the time, most of the time, or some of the time? Write down their exact answer and circle one of the options in the Frequency column.

Speaker	Remember?	Answer	Frequency
1	(Yes) No	Yeah.	(All the time) Most of the time Some of the time
2	Yes No		All the time Most of the time Some of the time
3	Yes No		All the time Most of the time Some of the time

(Continued)

Speaker	Remember?	Answer	Frequency
4	Yes No		All the time Most of the time Some of the time
5	Yes No		All the time Most of the time Some of the time
6	Yes No		All the time Most of the time Some of the time

C. Listening for Specific Ideas. Video/Audio   Listen again to some of the speakers describe their dreams. Listen for the answers to these questions.

1. Speaker 1: What did she do in Japan?

_____

_____

2. Speaker 3: What kind of dreams does she usually remember?

_____

_____

3. Speaker 4: What happened to the papers on her desk?

_____

_____

4. Speaker 5: What did he dream about?

_____

_____

After Listening

A. Talking about Dreams. (Group)   Discuss this question and write your answers in the chart.

- In Part One, you read about a common dream theme, flying. In the interview, Speaker 4 describes a dream about snakes. What are some other common dream themes and symbols?

Add them to the chart in the Common Dream Themes and Symbols column. Then talk about possible interpretations for each of the dream themes. Think about psychological interpretations, cultural or folk interpretations, and common sense interpretations. Write your ideas in the Possible Interpretations column.

Common Dream Themes and Symbols	Possible Interpretations
Flying	Desire for freedom
Snakes	Fear of animals
Losing a tooth	Losing a friend

B. Interpreting Dreams. (Group)   You are going to **make up** (invent) a dream. Then you will describe your dream to another group. Finally, you will listen to the other group's dream and give your interpretation of it.

Step One

In your group, create a **dream scenario** (description). Use typical dream themes and symbols. Use the ideas from your discussion in Exercise A. Make your group's dream as fantastic, strange, or scary as you want. Use your imagination. Write it down or write enough details so that you can describe it later.

Step Two

Choose one group member to describe the dream to the class. As you listen to each group's dream, take notes.

Step Three

Use your notes to interpret each group's dream that you heard. Refer to the chart you made in Exercise A for interpretation ideas. Choose a different group member to present your group's interpretation to the class.

Step Four

Now vote on the best interpretation for each dream.

Part Three   The Mechanics of Listening and Speaking

Language Function

Avoiding Answering Questions `Audio`

Sometimes you don't want to answer a question that someone asks you. There are many reasons not to answer a question: It seems impolite to you; it makes you uncomfortable; you're not sure how to answer it; or you simply don't have time to answer it. Here are some ways to avoid answering questions:

Example: A: May I ask you a question? Do you remember your dreams?

B: I'd rather not answer that.

I'd prefer not to answer.

I'm not interested in discussing that.

That's personal.

Sorry, I don't have time.

A. Practice. `Audio`   Listen to and read the following questions. These are the kinds of questions many people don't want to answer. After you hear each question, use one of the answers in the box above to avoid answering it.

1. How much do you weigh?

_____

2. How much money do you earn?

_____

3. May I ask you a question? What kind of dreams do you usually have?

_____

4. What score did you get on the TOEFL exam?

_____

5. Do you mind if I ask you a question? What is your religion?

_____

6. How old are you?

_____

7. May I ask you a question? Are you married?

_____

8. Why don't you have any children?

_____

Pronunciation

Can vs. Can't **Audio**

It's sometimes difficult to hear the difference between _can_ and _can't,_ especially when people speak quickly. However, in statements, most people shorten the vowel sound in _can_ and lengthen it in _can't._

Listen to these examples:

/ə/	/æ/
A: You <u>can</u> come with us if you want.	B: Sorry, I <u>can't</u>. I've got homework.
A: Sure, you <u>can</u> say that.	B: No, you <u>can't</u> say that.

B. Practice. **Audio**   Check (✓) the statement that you hear.

1. _____ You can ask me that question.

_____ You can't ask me that question.

2. _____ I can see over your head.

_____ I can't see over your head.

3. _____ She can come with us.

_____ She can't come with us.

4. _____ Mike can read without his glasses.

_____ Mike can't read without his glasses.

5. _____ I can understand French.

_____ I can't understand French.

6. _____ They can hear you.

_____ They can't hear you.

C. Practice. (Pair)   Now practice saying *can* and *can't* so that your partner can tell the difference. Say either statement *a* or *b*. Your partner will circle the letter of the statement he or she hears. Check to be sure the correct one is circled. Then switch roles.

1. *a.* You can ask me that question.   *b.* You can't ask me that question.

2. *a.* I can see over your head.   *b.* I can't see over your head.

3. *a.* She can come with us.   *b.* She can't come with us.

4. *a.* Mike can read without his glasses.   *b.* Mike can't read without his glasses.

5. *a.* I can understand French.   *b.* I can't understand French.

6. *a.* They can hear you.   *b.* They can't hear you.

Pronunciation

Verbs Ending in *–ed* (Audio)

The *-ed* verb ending is pronounced as an extra syllable /ɪd/, or as /t/ or /d/ at the end of the simple past form or the past participle form of a verb. The pronunciation of *-ed** depends on the last *sound* of the simple form of the verb:

1. Pronounce *–ed* as an extra syllable /ɪd/ when the simple form of the verb ends in a /t/ or /d/ sound.

    Here is an example:

    /t/   **/d/**
    wai<u>t</u> – waited   lan<u>d</u> – landed

2. Pronounce *-ed* as /t/ when the simple form of the verb ends with a voiceless consonant sound (/f/, /k/, /p/, /s/, /ʃ/, /tʃ/, /ks/).

    Here are some examples:

    lau<u>gh</u> – laughed (gh = /f/)   cra<u>sh</u> – crashed (sh = /ʃ/)
    wal<u>k</u> – walked   wat<u>ch</u> – watched (ch = /tʃ/)
    wra<u>p</u> – wrapped   fa<u>x</u> – faxed (x = /ks/)
    mi<u>ss</u> – missed

*Note: The pronunciation of *-ed* depends on the last *sound* of the simple form of the verb, not on the last letter.

3. Pronounce *-ed* as /d/ when the simple form of the verb ends with a voiced consonant sound (/b/, /g/, /dʒ/, /m/, /n/, /ŋ/, /l/, /r/, /ʒ/, /v/, /z/) or a vowel sound.

Here are some examples:

describe – described   call – called

brag – bragged   order – ordered

judge – judged (dg = dʒ)   bathe – bathed (th = /ʒ/)

name – named   wave – waved

rain – rained   buzz – buzzed

bang – banged (ng = /ŋ/)   play – played

D. Practice. **Audio**   Listen to the following simple past verbs. Do you hear /ɪd/, /t/, or /d/? Check (✓) the pronunciation that you hear. Use the rules you learned on pages 158–159 to help you decide. (You'll hear each verb two times.)

	/ɪd/	/t/	/d/			/ɪd/	/t/	/d/
1. studied					10. called			
2. ripped					11. molded			
3. raided					12. looked			
4. hitched					13. traded			
5. aimed					14. sprayed			
6. weaved					15. skated			
7. agreed					16. washed			
8. camped					17. weighed			
9. weeded					18. asked			

E. Practice. **Audio**   Repeat each word after the speaker.

/ɪd/	/t/	/d/
molded	washed	weighed
skated	hitched	sprayed
traded	camped	called
weeded	ripped	agreed

F. Practice. **Pair**   Decide on the pronunciation of these words. Write /ɪd/, /t/, or /d/ in the blank. Then practice saying them with a partner.

_____	**1.** turned	_____	**8.** interviewed	_____	**15.** pressed
_____	**2.** pointed	_____	**9.** evaluated	_____	**16.** dreamed
_____	**3.** thanked	_____	**10.** switched	_____	**17.** heat
_____	**4.** appreciated	_____	**11.** sewed	_____	**18.** clothed
_____	**5.** valued	_____	**12.** kissed	_____	**19.** sailed
_____	**6.** admired	_____	**13.** analyzed	_____	**20.** changed
_____	**7.** questioned	_____	**14.** waited	_____	**21.** headed

G. Practice. **Group**   Now use words with the three sounds of the *-ed* ending (/t/, /d/, and /ɪd/) in conversations. Interview your classmates. Use the following questions or use the words in the list in the exercises on pages 159–160 to make up your own. Write your classmates' names on a chart like the one below. Which student collects the most names?

Example: A: Have you ever ask<u>ed</u> someone an embarrassing question?

B: No.

Find someone who . . .	Names
has ever interview<u>ed</u> a famous person	
has ever ask<u>ed</u> someone an embarrassing question	
has ever wait<u>ed</u> in line to see a movie	
has ever analy<u>zed</u> someone else's dreams	
has ever collect<u>ed</u> stamps as a hobby	
has ever sail<u>ed</u> across an ocean	
has ever camp<u>ed</u> on a beach	

Review: Language Functions

Asking a Question and Avoiding Answering a Question `Video/Audio`

Listen to these examples of how to ask a question and of how to avoid answering a question. You'll use these functions in the next section.

Put It Together

A. What's an Impolite Question? `Pair`   Some questions are appropriate if a close friend asks them, but not if a stranger asks them. For example, you might tell a friend how much you weigh, but not someone you've just met. Also, some questions are polite in one situation, but not in another. For example, a friend can ask you in private what you did on your date last night, but he or she shouldn't ask about such things in front of the class. Finally, questions that are polite in one culture may be considered impolite in another. For example, in some countries, it's OK to ask people how much money they make, but in the United States, this is considered a rude question.

Discuss the answers to these questions with your partner.

1. What questions can be polite or impolite, depending on who is asking them?

2. What questions can be polite or impolite, depending on the situation?

3. What questions may be polite in some countries, but are rude in the United States?

4. What questions may be polite in the United States, but are rude in other countries?

Write your ideas on the chart on page 162.

Topic	Polite? In Which Situation or Culture?	Impolite? In Which Situation or Culture?
Weight	If a friend asks in private.	If a stranger asks anyone in public.

B. Asking and (Not) Answering Questions. (Pair)   Now take turns asking questions and avoiding answering questions. Get ideas for questions from the topics in the chart you made in Exercise A. Use the statements for avoiding answering questions in the box on page 156. Pay attention to the pronunciation of *can* and *can't,* if applicable.

Part Four Broadcast English: Why Do We Sleep?

Before Listening

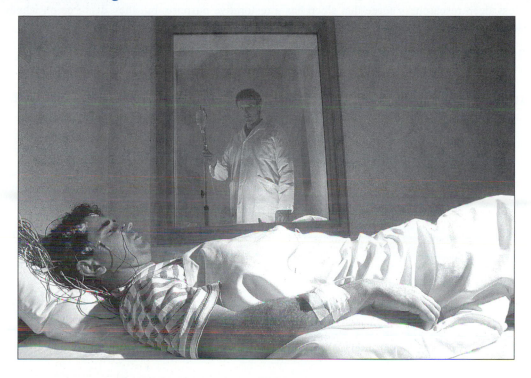

A. Thinking Ahead. **Group**   You are going to listen to a radio program about one theory on why we sleep. Before you listen, talk about sleep. Discuss the answers to these questions.

1. Why do we sleep, in your opinion?

2. About what percent of our lives do we spend asleep?

3. What do you think happens if a person doesn't get enough sleep?

B. Predicting. **Pair**   Before you listen, make a prediction about what you are going to hear. Discuss the answer to this question.

- Does the latest theory on sleep and dreaming say that dreaming is a message from our unconscious minds or just a result of brain activity while we sleep?

C. Guessing Meaning from Context.   In the radio program, you are going to hear some words that may be new to you. Before you listen, guess the meaning of some of the words from the program. The words are underlined in the sentences. Look for clues to their meaning in the words around them.

Write your guess in the blank after each sentence. Then check your guess with your teacher or the dictionary.

1. Most sleep researchers agree that sleep has a <u>restorative</u> purpose, but they disagree on whether sleep refreshes the mind or the body.

    Guess: _____

2. The basketball player's energy was completely <u>depleted</u> after the big game so she drank a lot of juice to restore it.

    Guess: _____

3. "You're trying to <u>deprive</u> us of a good night's sleep," Joe told his noisy neighbors. "Your loud music is going to keep us awake all night."

    Guess: _____

4. My energy <u>reserves</u> are low, but I'll restore them if I eat something.

    Guess: _____

5. He's a good <u>mimic</u>; he can imitate Mickey Mouse perfectly!

    Guess: _____

6. <u>Glucose</u> is a natural form of sugar in food that the body uses.

    Guess: _____

7. He spends the <u>bulk</u> of his time—about eight hours a day—working on his novel.

    Guess: _____

D. Vocabulary Preparation: Idioms and Phrasal Verbs.   There are many idiomatic expressions and phrasal verbs in the radio program. How many of them do you know? First, read each sentence and guess the meaning of the underlined words. Then choose their meaning from the definitions in the box. Write the letter in the blanks.

Definitions

a. use up (deplete) power or energy

b. use up (deplete) supplies

c. in your imagination

d. doing the right thing

e. figured out; solved

Sentences

_____ **1.** It took them many years to understand the code, but they finally <u>cracked</u> it.

_____ **2.** I was having trouble solving the problem, but I'm <u>on the right track</u> now.

_____ **3.** She's not really angry with you—it's <u>all in your head</u>!

_____ **4.** If you leave the lights on overnight in your car, you'll <u>run down</u> the battery.

_____ **5.** Whenever I have a big term paper to turn in, I <u>run out of</u> paper. Then I have to go to the office supply store.

academic Strategy

Understanding Literal and Figurative Language

Many words and expressions in English have two meanings, a **literal** meaning and a **figurative** meaning. The literal meaning of a word is its main meaning. It is usually the first definition of the word in the dictionary. The figurative meaning of a word is a meaning other than its usual meaning. It often makes a word picture or a comparison. For example, look at the word "sweet":

Literal meaning: containing sugar. I can't drink this coffee because it's too <u>sweet</u>.

Figurative meaning: nice or kind. I like our new neighbor—she's very <u>sweet</u>.

Practice.   Here is a sentence from the radio program. Is the underlined word used literally or figuratively?

There's a chemical in the brain called adenosine that's released when brain energy <u>stores</u> are depleted.

E. Vocabulary Preparation: Literal and Figurative Language.   The announcer in the radio
program uses some expressions in a figurative sense. Look at the literal definitions of the following
expressions. Then look at some sentences from the program. Decide if the underlined word is used
literally or figuratively.

1. **nightmare**

    Literal meaning: a bad dream

    Figurative meaning: a bad experience

    > If they are on the right track, it could open up entirely new ways of manipulating
    > sleep and treating the tens of millions of people in this country for whom getting a
    > good night's sleep is a <u>nightmare</u>.

    Literal or figurative? _____

2. **road**

    Literal meaning: a street or track for wheeled vehicles such as cars

    Figurative meaning: a way or means of reaching a goal

    > So dreaming is not so much a <u>road</u> to the unconscious as a <u>road</u> to continued
    > restorative sleep.

    Literal or figurative? _____

3. **expensive**

    Literal meaning: costing a lot of money

    Figurative meaning: using up anything that is valuable

    > Rekshofen agrees that sleep must have an important role for animals to be willing to
    > undertake such an <u>expensive</u> behavior.

    Literal or figurative? _____

Listening

A. Listening for the Main Idea.   (Audio)   Listen to the radio program. As you listen, try to answer
this question:

- According to sleep researcher Craig Heller's theory, why do we sleep?

listening Strategy

Understanding Scientific Terms **Audio**

In a radio or TV program about a technical or scientific subject, the announcer usually defines or explains difficult terms for the audience. Often the explanation is general or simplified, because you don't have to know the exact definition in order to understand the main ideas of the program. It's important not to worry when you don't understand a scientific term exactly. For example, the announcer in the radio program says:

"There's a chemical in the brain called <u>adenosine</u> that's released when energy stores are depleted."

In this case, you might not know exactly what adenosine is, but you do know that it's a chemical in the brain. That's all you need to know to understand the program.

B. Listening for Scientific Definitions. **Audio**   Listen to parts of the program. This time, listen for explanations of the following scientific terms. Then write in your own words what you think the terms mean.

Scientific Terms			
glycogen	glial cells	non-REM sleep	REM sleep

All you need to know is that

• glycogen is _____

• glial cells are _____

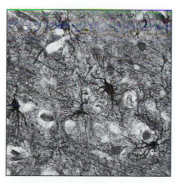

Glial cells

All you need to know is that

• non-REM sleep is _____

• REM sleep is _____

 *listening* **Strategy**

Understanding Analogies **Audio**

Speakers often use analogies to help listeners understand something technical or complicated. An analogy is a kind of comparison. For example, to explain the importance of good nutrition, someone might say, "Your body is like a car. It needs fuel to run properly." The speaker is making an analogy between a human body and a car.

C. Listening for an Analogy. **Audio**   Listen to another part of the program. This time, listen to the speaker make an analogy to explain something. The analogy is to a kind of machine. What is the machine? Circle your guess:

> *a.* a washing machine   *b.* a car   *c.* a computer

D. Listening for Details. **Audio**   Listen to another part of the program. Listen for details that answer these questions.

1. When we sleep, do we spend more time in REM sleep or non-REM sleep?

_____

2. When does the brain restore its glycogen reserves, during REM sleep or non-REM sleep?

_____

3. Does sleep researcher Alan Rekshofen agree with Heller and Bennington's theory?

_____

4. Why does Alan Rekshofen say that sleeping is an expensive behavior?

_____

academic Strategy

Separating Fact from Theory Audio

In the radio program you have listened to, you heard a new theory about sleep. In these types of programs, it's important to separate facts from theories. The difference between facts and theories is whether or not they can be proven. In other words, facts are things that are true or have been proven. On the other hand, theories are reasonable ideas based on fact, but have not been proven. You can distinguish theories from facts by paying attention to some verbal cues. For example, people present (or should present) theories with verbs such as *propose, think,* and *believe.* They might also introduce a theoretical statement with *perhaps,* or use modals such as *might* and *may* within the statement.

Here are some examples:

- Some scientists <u>think</u> that fallout from an asteroid created a climate change that eventually extinguished the dinosaur population.

- Dinosaurs <u>may</u> have become extinct because of an asteroid.

Practice.   Listen to some statements from the radio program. Check (✓) *Fact* if the speaker presents the information as a fact. Check (✓) *Theory* if the speaker presents it as a theory.

Statement	Fact	Theory
1	☐	☐
2	☐	☐
3	☐	☐
4	☐	☐

After Listening

Discussion. Group   Discuss the answers to these questions.

1. Why are scientists so interested in sleep?

2. According to sleep researcher Craig Heller's theory, why do we sleep?

3. Why do we dream, according to Heller and Bennington?

4. Explain in your own words what Alan Rekshofen means when he says that sleeping is an "expensive behavior."

5. Do you agree with Heller and Bennington's theory? Why or why not?

. : : : : : **Part Five** Academic English: Sleep
and Dreaming

Before Listening

A. Discussion. (Group)   You are going to listen to a lecture about sleep and dreaming. Before you listen, discuss the answers to these questions.

1. What happens to your body when you're asleep? What happens to your brain?

2. What happens if you don't get enough sleep?

3. What happens to your body when you're dreaming? What happens to your brain?

4. What are some scientific theories on why we dream?

B. Thinking Ahead.   Look at the outline for the lecture on pages 172–176 and think about your discussion in Exercise A. What would you like to know about sleep and dreaming? Write at least three questions about the subject.

_____

_____

_____

C. Guessing Meaning from Context.   In the lecture, you are going to hear some words that may be new to you. Before you listen, guess the meaning of some words from the lecture. The words are underlined in the sentences. Look for clues to their meaning in the words around them.

Write your guess in the blank after each sentence. Then check your guess with your teacher or the dictionary.

1. He's very <u>moody</u> today: one minute he's happy and the next he's depressed.

   Guess: _____

2. This new exercise routine will <u>rejuvenate</u> you; you'll feel like a teenager in a few weeks.

   Guess: _____

3. When an animal is in <u>hibernation</u>, it's in a state that is like sleep and it needs very little food.

   Guess: _____

4. Heller and Bennington believe that the purpose of sleep is <u>cerebral</u> restoration; that is, they think the brain needs to shut down to restore itself.

   Guess: _____

5. The <u>cortex</u> is the gray matter that covers the outside of the brain.

   Guess: _____

6. Researchers use an electroencephalograph (EEG) to measure waves that the brain <u>emits</u>, or sends out, during sleep.

   Guess: _____

7. I used to know the capitals of every state in the United States, but I can <u>recall</u> only a few of them now.

   Guess: _____

Listening

A. Listening for Main Ideas. **Audio** Listen to the lecture one time. Don't take notes. Don't worry about understanding everything. Just listen for the main idea. As you listen, try to answer these questions:

- What are some explanations for why we sleep?

- What happens to our bodies when we are dreaming?

B. Listening for the Meaning of New Words and Expressions. **Audio** Listen to these words and expressions in sentences from the lecture. Then write the definition you hear.

1. consciousness = _____

2. an altered state of consciousness = _____

3. incoherent = _____

4. circadian rhythms = _____

5. EEGs (electroencephalographs) = _____

C. Taking Notes: Using an Outline. <Audio> Listen to the lecture and fill in as much of the outline as you can. Start at the beginning. The main topics and subtopics are already in the outline. Write the details that support each subtopic. Don't worry if you can't fill in much. You'll listen to the lecture again.

Sleep and Dreaming

I. Consciousness

    A. Consciousness is ___the state of being aware_____

        1. Humans use senses to _____

        2. Humans can use any or all senses. For example: _____

        _____

    B. Human consciousness is _____

        1. Humans have the capacity _____

        2. Humans can _____

II. Sleep

    A. Sleep is _____

        1. Experts know that the longer someone goes without sleep, _____

        _____

        Without sleep: _____

        a. People have difficulty _____

        b. They have _____

        c. They get _____

        d. With prolonged sleeplessness, people become _____

        _____

        2. Record for person staying awake: _____

        _____

    B. The cycle of sleep: Circadian rhythms

        1. Sleep is a _____

        a. Our bodies have a biological need to _____

        b. Our bodies' natural biological need for rest is _____

        c. This natural rhythm is known as _____

        _____

2. Some researchers describe circadian rhythms as _____

_____

3. One internal clock controls _____

4. The second internal clock controls _____

_____

5. Some researchers describe circadian rhythms as _____

_____

6. Circadian rhythms have these features:

a. _____

b. _____

c. _____

d. _____

7. Our natural circadian rhythms may be disturbed by _____

_____

C. Sleep: A process of rest or recovery? Three perspectives:

1. _____

2. _____

3. _____

D. Why do some people need more sleep than others?

1. Everybody requires some sleep.

2. Most people require _____

3. An individual's sleep needs vary from _____

4. _____ sleep longer than _____ , the

_____ sleep less than young people

5. _____ do not influence the amount of sleep people need.

E. Cycles and stages of sleep

1. Our sleep cycles are _____

2. A full sleep cycle lasts approximately _____

3. The average sleep pattern (eight hours) has _____

4. Using EEGs, researchers have _____

5. Four stages of sleep

   a. Stage 1: _____

   b. Stages 2 and 3: _____

   c. Stage 4: _____

F. REM and non-REM sleep

  1. REM and non-REM sleep

    a. Rapid eye movement (REM) sleep is _____

    _____

    b. _____ identifies REM sleep

    c. REM sleep is the moments during sleep when we _____

    _____

    d. REM sleep begins after _____

    e. REM sleep is necessary for _____

    _____

    f. Non-rapid eye movement (non-REM) sleep is _____

    _____

  2. Alpha and delta waves

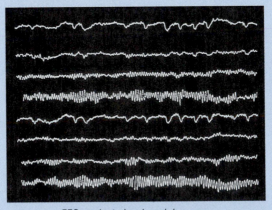

EEG readout showing alpha waves

    a. The brain emits alpha waves _____

    _____

    b. The brain emits delta waves _____

    c. The brain emits intense wave activity during _____

   _____

G. Sleep deprivation: Going without REM sleep

   1. People who are denied REM sleep are _____

   and become _____

   2. People who are denied REM sleep for a considerable amount of time _____

   _____

   3. People who sleep, but are denied REM sleep _____

   _____

III. Dreams

   A. What is a dream?

     1. A dream is _____

     2. Dreams begin _____

     3. A dream includes _____

     4. A dream can include _____

     5. During dreams:

       a. _____ is increased

       b. _____ occur

       c. _____ can be identified

       d. _____ is minimal

     6. Non-REM sleep is _____

     7. Most people have _____ dreams per night.

     8. Dreams last from _____ to _____

   B. Why do we remember some but not all our dreams?

     1. We have _____ each night, yet only remember

     _____

     2. Some people have _____

     3. Most dreams are about _____

     4. Most dreams include _____

5. Most dreams have common themes including _____

_____

6. Sounds and other sensations that do not wake up a sleeper _____

_____

7. We remember a dream if _____

8. We remember dreams by our pattern of awakening:

    a. People who _____ remember more dreams

    b. People who _____ remember fewer dreams

C. Lucid dreaming

  1. Lucid dreaming is _____

  2. Lucid dreaming makes you feel _____

_____; can be

_____

D. The meaning of dreams

  1. Many cultures and traditions _____

_____

  2. In Western culture, _____

_____

  3. Other researchers believe _____

    a. During sleep _____

_____

    b. The brain's _____

_____

Now listen again. Fill in any missing information in the outline.

listening **Strategy**

Listening for Topic Change Signals `Audio`

Speakers often use signals to help the audience pay attention to a lecture. Listening to these signals will help you take notes and organize them well.

1. Speakers sometimes move away from the topic when giving a lecture. This is called a **digression.** They often give the audience a signal when they do this.

    Here are some examples:

    -   By the way . . .
    -   That reminds me . . .

2. Speakers also signal the audience when they return to the topic.

    Here are some examples:

    -   As I was saying . . .
    -   Getting back to what I was saying . . .
    -   Moving on . . .

3. In addition, speakers sometimes signal the audience when they are going to introduce the next subtopic of the lecture.

    Here are some examples:

    -   (Now) Let's take a look at . . .
    -   Let's turn our attention to . . .
    -   This brings us to the topic of . . .

D. Listening for Signals. `Audio`   Listen for signals like the ones in the box above. Write the signal in the blank and indicate the purpose of each one: moving off the topic, returning to the topic, or introducing a new subtopic.

1. _____

2. _____

3. _____

After Listening

Using Your Notes. **Group**   Use your notes to discuss these questions about the lecture.

1. What are some explanations for why we sleep?

2. What are the four sleep stages?

3. What happens if you don't get enough sleep?

4. What happens to our bodies when we are dreaming?

5. What are some cures for sleeplessness?

 Step Beyond

Giving a Presentation.   You are going to give a short presentation (three to five minutes) to the class or to a small group of classmates on an aspect of sleep or dreaming that interests you.

Step One

Pick a subject related to sleep or dreaming that interests you. Some possibilities might include the following:

- a recent theory (or theories) on why we sleep

- a recent theory (or theories) on why we dream

- dream interpretation

  a. cultural or folk beliefs about the meaning of dreams

  b. psychological theories on what dreams mean

  c. a description of one of your (or someone else's) dreams and what you think the dream means

- remedies for sleeplessness

- a summary of a news article, website, or radio or TV program on sleep and dreaming and your opinion of it

Step Two

Do library or Web research on your topic. Take notes.

speaking Strategy

Asking Questions and Keeping the Audience in Mind

You saw how speakers use signals when they give a lecture. Another way speakers signal the audience is by asking questions. This not only signals the organization of the lecture, it also helps keep the audience interested. Some examples of questions from the lecture on sleep and dreaming that you heard include the following:

- What are the cycles and stages of sleep?
- So, why do we sleep?
- What is a dream?

A similar technique is to imagine what the audience might think about the topic. For example, in the lecture on sleep and dreaming, the speaker says:

- You might wonder why we remember some, but not all, of our dreams.
- We often wonder why some people need more sleep than others do.

Step Three

Prepare a presentation from your notes. Practice your presentation. Think about ways to use signals and questions to keep the audience's interests in mind, and to help your listeners pay attention. Write some of these down on your note cards so you remember to use them when you speak.

Step Four

Give your presentation. Use your notes; don't read. (See Chapter Four, page 143.) Make eye contact as you speak and keep your audience in mind.

Step Five

Evaluate each other's presentations. For each presenter ask these questions:

✓ Did the speaker use notes to make the presentation (rather than reading)?

✓ Did the speaker make eye contact with the audience?

✓ Did the speaker use signals or questions to help the audience pay attention?

chapter *Six*

Abnormal Psychology

In this chapter, you'll listen to information about abnormal behavior such as paranoia. You'll also discuss fears and other anxiety disorders.

• • : : : : **Part One** Introduction: What Is Abnormal Behavior?

A. Predicting. **Pair**   You are going to read some definitions of abnormal behavior. Before you read, look at the following descriptions of different kinds of behavior. Discuss these behaviors with a partner. Say whether each is normal or abnormal, in your opinion. Check (✓) the appropriate column.

Behaviors	Normal	Abnormal
1. A woman cheats on her income taxes.		
2. A man takes ten showers a day.		
3. A man cannot get or keep a job, and lives on the streets.		
4. A woman lives alone and has no friends.		
5. A man believes that he is Napoleon.		
6. A woman is afraid of flying in an airplane.		
7. A woman claims that aliens from outer space communicate with her through her television.		
8. A man didn't cry at his mother's funeral.		

B. Thinking Ahead. **Pair** Before you read, discuss the answers to these questions.

1. Have you ever seen anyone whose behavior seemed abnormal to you? Describe the behavior.

2. How do you define abnormal behavior?

What Is Abnormal Behavior?

For nine months, 54-year-old Richard Thompson's home was a downtown storm **drain** (sewer) in San Diego, California. The city does not allow people to live in sewers, and **evicted** Thompson (forced him to leave). Although he has lived in several care centers and mental hospitals, Thompson prefers the privacy and the comfort of the sewer.

The question is: Is Thompson's behavior abnormal? We can take three approaches in answering this question.

Statistical Frequency

According to the statistical frequency approach, a behavior is considered abnormal if it occurs infrequently compared to the behaviors of most people. By this definition, living in a sewer would be considered abnormal. However, so would getting a Ph.D., raising orchids, being president, or living in a monastery, since relatively few people do these things. As these last examples show, the statistical frequency definition of abnormality isn't too useful.

Deviation from Social Norms

According to the social norms approach, a behavior is considered abnormal if it **deviates** (is very different) from **social norms** (what is OK in a particular society). Because Thompson greatly deviated from society's norms when he decided to live in a sewer, his behavior would be considered abnormal. However, a

Richard Thompson lived happily in a San Diego sewer until he was evicted by the city.

definition of abnormality based only on being different from social norms doesn't work when social norms change with time. For example, 30 years ago, smoking was considered a sign of a mature, sophisticated person; today people think of it as a serious health risk. Thirty years ago, a woman who was thin was considered to be ill; today many women work very hard to be thin. So you can see that defining abnormality on the basis of social norms is difficult because these norms may and do change over time.

Maladaptive Behavior

According to the maladaptive behavior approach, a behavior may be defined as abnormal if it interferes with an individual's ability

to function as a person or in a society. For example, being afraid to go out in public, hear-
45 ing voices that make you do dangerous things, feeling compelled to wash your hands for hours on end, starving yourself to death, and committing mass murder would all be considered maladaptive and, in that sense, abnormal.

50 However, Thompson's seemingly successful adaptation to living in a sewer may not be maladaptive for him, and certainly has no adverse consequences to society. Of the three definitions discussed here, most mental health pro-
55 fessionals would agree that the maladaptive definition is perhaps the most useful.

Source: Rod Plotnik, "What Is Abnormal Behavior?" adapted from *Introduction to Psychology, Third Edition.* Copyright © 1993 by Wadsworth, Inc. Adapted and reprinted with the permission of Brooks/Cole Publishing Company, a division of Thomson Publishing Inc., 511 Forest Lodge Road, Pacific Grove, CA 93950-5040.

C. Comprehension Check. Group   Discuss the answers to these questions.

1. Why is there no single definition of abnormal behavior?

2. What are the three definitions of abnormal behavior, according to the article? Outline them by completing the following chart.

Definition	Describe It in Your Own Words	Give an Example
1		
2		
3		

3. According to the article, which definition of abnormal behavior would most people agree with?

4. Look again at your classification of the behaviors in Exercise A, page 182. Using the definitions of abnormal behavior you have seen in the reading, reclassify each item as normal or abnormal. Did you change any classifications?

5. Are there cultural differences in defining abnormal behavior? Give examples to support your answer.

D. Response Writing.   Choose *one* of these topics. Write about it for ten minutes. Don't worry about grammar and don't use a dictionary. Just put as many ideas as you can on paper.

• What is your definition of abnormal behavior? Has it changed at all after reading the article?

• Describe someone's behavior that you think is abnormal.

• Describe some cultural differences in defining abnormal behavior. Give examples to support your answer.

Part Two   Everyday English: What Are You Afraid of? (Interview)

Before Listening

A. Thinking Ahead.   **Pair**   You are going to listen to Chrissy interview people on the street. She's going to ask them what they are afraid of. Before you listen, discuss the answers to these questions.

1. What are you afraid of? Do you ever experience "irrational" fears?

2. What fears are "normal"?

3. What fears are "abnormal"? In other words, what fears might **disrupt** (cause serious problems in) a person's daily life?

B. Predicting.   **Group**   You are going to listen to six people answer the question: "What are you afraid of?" What do you think that most people will say? Do most people have fears? What kinds of things do you think they'll say they are afraid of? In your groups, make predictions.

C. Vocabulary Preparation.   The people in the interview use some words and expressions that may be new to you. First, read each sentence and guess the meaning of the underlined words. Then choose their meaning from the definitions in the box. Write the letter in the blanks.

> **Definitions**
>
> *a.* slippery   *c.* partly, but not completely
>
> *b.* strange; unusual   *d.* recovered from

Sentences

_____ 1. I used to know the names of all the countries in Africa, but I've <u>sort of</u> forgotten them now.

_____ 2. Sheryl used to be afraid of flying, but she's <u>gotten over</u> it with the help of a psychiatrist.

_____ 3. I used to have <u>weird</u> dreams, but now they're not very exciting.

_____ 4. I hate the feel of seaweed when I swim in the ocean because it's so <u>slimy</u>.

Listening

A. Listening for the Main Idea. (Video/Audio)   Now listen to the interview. As you listen, try to answer this question:

• Do all the speakers have some kind of fear?

B. Listening for Details. (Video/Audio)   Listen to the interview again. This time, fill in the chart with the following information about each speaker.

• What is the speaker afraid of?

• If the speaker gives a reason for the fear, what is it?

Speaker	Fear	Reason
1		
2		
3		
4		
5		
6		
7		

C. Listening for Specific Information. (Video/Audio) Listen again to some of the speakers describe their fears. Listen for the answers to these questions.

1. Speaker 1: Is she still afraid of spiders?

_____

2. Speaker 3: Did she almost drown as a child?

_____

3. Speaker 6: How does she describe seaweed?

_____

4. Speaker 7: How does she sound when she gives her answer? In other words, does she sound bored, confident, or uncertain?

_____

After Listening

A. Taking a Survey. (Group) As you heard in the interview, most people have mild fears that they don't mind talking about. You are going to interview three students in your class about their fears.

Step One

Discuss the answers to these questions in your groups.

1. Will most people discuss their fears? Do age or sex have anything to do with this?

2. What are the most common fears? Do age or sex have anything to do with this?

3. To what extent do common fears disrupt a person's life? Do age or sex have anything to do with this?

Then in your groups, create a list of common fears. Write your ideas in the blanks.

_____

_____

_____

Step Two

Now survey three students. If possible, talk to both males and females of different cultures and of different ages. Write their answers in the chart. If a person does *not* want to discuss his or her fears, that's OK. Find someone else. Write your own question.

Student Name Sex	Student 1 _____ ☐ Male ☐ Female	Student 2 _____ ☐ Male ☐ Female	Student 3 _____ ☐ Male ☐ Female
Part 1			
1. Are you willing to discuss your fears?	☐ Yes ☐ No	☐ Yes ☐ No	☐ Yes ☐ No
2. How old are you?			
Part 2			
3. Do you have any fears?	☐ Yes ☐ No	☐ Yes ☐ No	☐ Yes ☐ No
4. What, if anything, are you afraid of?			
5. Does this fear cause you any problems?	☐ Yes ☐ No	☐ Yes ☐ No	☐ Yes ☐ No
6. Write your own question here. _____ _____ _____ _____			

B. Discussing Survey Results. (Group)   Form small groups. Try not to be in a group with some-one that you interviewed. Discuss the results of your survey. Now that you have your results, use them to answer again the questions you discussed in Step One.

1. Were most people willing to discuss their fears? Do age or sex have anything to do with this?

2. What are the most common fears? Do age or sex have anything to do with this?

3. To what extent do fears cause problems in people's lives? Do age or sex have anything to do with this?

. . : : : : : :   Part Three   The Mechanics of Listening and Speaking

Language Function

Asking for Information Over the Phone   (Audio)

People often try to get as much information as they can over the phone before they go somewhere—this saves them time, energy, and sometimes money. Here are some ways to ask for information* over the phone:

A: Bright Lights Video. What can I do for you?

B: Hi. <u>Can you tell me if you have</u> *Star Wars?*

Yes, hello. <u>Do you have</u> *Star Wars?*

Uh yeah, hi. <u>Would you happen to have</u> a copy of *Star Wars?*

Uh, hi. <u>I was wondering if you have</u> *Star Wars.*

*Note: Depending on the information you want, you might also ask the following:

• <u>Do you sell</u> . . . ?

• <u>Do you carry</u> . . .?

A. Practice. (Audio)   Listen to the video store employee answer the phone. He will ask you what he can do for you. Ask for the following video titles using the expressions in the box on page 189.

Examples: A: Bright Lights Video. What can I do for you?

B: [You ask for *Casablanca.*] Yes. Hello. Do you have a copy of *Casablanca?*

A: Bright Lights Video. What can I do for you?

B: [You ask for *The Wizard of Oz.*] Yes. Hello. I was wondering if you have a copy of *The Wizard of Oz.*

1. [You ask for *E.T.*]

2. [You ask for *The Godfather.*]

3. [You ask for *Star Trek.*]

4. [You ask for *Dances with Wolves.*]

5. [You ask for *Alien.*]

6. [You ask for *Psycho.*]

Language Function

Asking Someone to Hold (Audio)

Sometimes you have to ask the person you're speaking to on the phone to **hold** (stay on the line while you go away from the phone) for various reasons. Here are some ways to do this:

A: Can you tell me if you have *Star Wars?*

B: Hang on a minute.   **Less Formal**

Hold on a minute. I'll check.

Can you hold?

Please hold.

Can you hold on for a minute?

Would you mind holding on for a minute?   **More Formal**

B. Practice. (Pair)   Practice asking your partner to hold. Student A asks for a movie. You can ask for the following ones, or use your own ideas. Student B asks student A to hold using one of the expressions in the box above. Then exchange roles.

Movies

Forrest Gump	*Mutiny on the Bounty*
Frankenstein	*Raiders of the Lost Ark*
King Kong	*The Great Dictator*

Pronunciation

/ɛ/ vs. /æ/ **Audio**

It is important to hear the difference between these two sounds: /ɛ/ and /æ/. Listen to these examples. Do you hear the difference?

/ɛ/	/æ/
Do you have a pen?	Do you have a pan?

Now listen to these examples:

/ɛ/	/æ/
bed	bad
send	sand
men	man
pen	pan
said	sad

Notice the different spellings for the /ɛ/ sound.

C. Practice. **Audio**   Listen to the following words. Circle the word that you hear.

1. said — sad
2. lend — land
3. pen — pan
4. trek — track
5. bend — band

6. send — sand
7. ten — tan
8. left — laughed
9. guess — gas
10. gem — jam

D. Practice. **Audio**   Check (✓) the statement that you hear.

1. _____ *a.* Can you send that for me?
   _____ *b.* Can you sand that for me?

2. _____ *a.* Did you see the gem?
   _____ *b.* Did you see the jam?

3. _____ *a.* Can I borrow your pen?
   _____ *b.* Can I borrow your pan?

4. _____ *a.* I bought ten shirts for the team.
   _____ *b.* I bought tan shirts for the team.

5. _____ *a.* He left when he heard the joke.
   _____ *b.* He laughed when he heard the joke.

6. _____ *a.* They drove around the bend.
   _____ *b.* They drove around the band.

E. Practice. (Pair) Say one of the statements from Exercise D. (Don't say them in order.) Your partner will write *a* or *b*. Check each statement to see if it matches. If your partner didn't write the correct letter, try again. Then exchange roles.

F. Practice. (Class) Now use words with the sounds /ɛ/ and /æ/ in conversations. Interview your classmates. Ask questions to fill in the chart or use the Word List that follows to make up your own. Write your classmates' names in the chart. Which student collects the most names?

Find someone who . . .	Names
likes to wear t<u>a</u>n clothes	
has been on a tr<u>e</u>k in the mountains	
plays in a b<u>a</u>nd	
has a favorite g<u>e</u>m	
knows how to s<u>a</u>nd wood	
eats j<u>a</u>m on toast	
is l<u>e</u>ft-handed	
g<u>ue</u>ss<u>e</u>s answers on the TOEFL exam	

Word List			
bed	bad	lend	land
bend	band	said	sad
gem	jam	send	sand
guess	gas	pen	pan
left	laughed	ten	tan

Review: Language Functions

Beginning and Ending a Phone Conversation and Asking for Information over the Phone `Video/Audio`

Listen to these examples of how to ask for information over the phone and tell someone to hold. You'll use these functions in the next section.

Put It Together

A. Whom Do You Call? `Pair`   Practice asking for information over the phone. First, discuss the most common situations in which you have to ask for information over the phone. Think of the places (people, services, businesses, organizations) that you call and the things that you ask for (items, help, information), and fill in the chart with your ideas.

Places	Things You Ask For
bookstore	book title
restaurant	menu items
clothing store	prices

B. Asking for Information Over the Phone. **Pair**   Take turns asking for information and giving information. Find ideas for questions from the information in your chart in Exercise A. If you are giving the information, ask the other person to hold, if applicable. Use the expressions for asking for information and asking someone to hold on pages 189 and 190. Pay attention to the /ɛ/ and /æ/ sounds.

Example: Bookstore clerk: Megabooks International. Can I help you?

                        Student: Uh, yeah. Do you have *Foundation,* by Isaac Asimov?

              Bookstore clerk: Uh, hold on a minute . . . I'll check.

                        Student: Thanks.

. . : : : : **Part Four** Broadcast English: What Is Paranoia?

Before Listening

A. Thinking Ahead. **Group**   You are going to listen to a radio program about **paranoia,** a kind of mental illness that has a basis in fear. Before you listen, talk about fear. Discuss the answers to these questions.

1. The program was recorded in the late 1990s. A frightening crime trend in the '90s was drive-by shootings (people in cars shooting other cars or people on the street for no apparent reason). What are some real things that people fear in today's world? Think about natural disasters, new diseases, crime, etc.

2. Why are people afraid of certain things? What purpose does fear serve?

B. Predicting. <Pair> Before you listen, make a prediction about what you are going to hear. Discuss the answer to this question.

• Is there an effective treatment for paranoia?

C. Guessing Meaning from Context. Before you listen to the radio program, guess the meaning of some of the words from the program. The words are underlined in the sentences. Look for clues to their meaning in the words around them.

Write your guess in the blank after each sentence. Then check your guess with your teacher or the dictionary.

1. Edvard Munch's painting *The Scream* <u>evokes</u> a very definite feeling—it expresses the feeling of fear and anxiety.

    Guess: _____

2. According to Ronald Siegel, the basis for paranoia is <u>lurking</u> deep inside everyone's brain; it only comes to the surface and becomes a problem when you have trouble dealing with the fears of the everyday world.

    Guess: _____

3. Very upsetting experiences can act as <u>triggers</u> that cause "normal" people to suddenly act abnormally.

    Guess: _____

4. He takes a drug that <u>activates</u> a certain part of his brain. This stimulation helps him pay better attention in class.

    Guess: _____

5. I used to get very <u>agitated</u> when I watched the evening news; it made me so upset that I decided not to watch it any more.

    Guess: _____

6. She has a <u>deep-seated</u> fear of flying: She's had it all her life, she doesn't understand the cause, and she can't get rid of it.

    Guess: _____

7. I have a sense of <u>unease</u> about this trip; I'm afraid something will go wrong.

    Guess: _____

8. There has been a <u>resurgence</u> in the number of paranoia cases we've seen at this hospital; there haven't been as many cases since the late 1980s.

Guess: _____

9. If a person has a <u>neurological</u> problem, it means that he or she has a problem with brain function.

Guess: _____

10. The <u>limbic system</u> is the primitive part of the brain that controls basic functions such as emotion and motivation.

Guess: _____

11. Fear about crime, disease, and natural disasters was <u>pervasive</u> in California in the '90s; it affected many people around the state.

Guess: _____

D. Vocabulary Preparation: Figurative Language.   The speaker in the radio program uses some words figuratively. (See Chapter Five, page 165.) First, read each sentence and guess the meaning of the underlined words. Then choose their meaning from the definitions in the box. Write the letter in the blanks.

> **Definitions**
>
> *a.* destroy   *d.* take control of
>
> *b.* negative feeling   *e.* become extremely influenced by a feeling
>
> *c.* uncovered, exposed

Sentences

_____ **1.** Sometimes unreasonable fears can <u>grip</u> you, and you can't do anything about them.

_____ **2.** Acidic foods are bad for you because they <u>eat away</u> your tooth enamel.

_____ **3.** Even though I'm afraid of crime in the city, I'm not going to <u>get carried away</u> about it and become too paranoid to go out of the house!

_____ **4.** The <u>demon</u> of paranoia has affected many famous people throughout history such as Adolf Hitler and Ernest Hemingway.

_____ **5.** His emotions have been very <u>raw</u> ever since he witnessed that terrible accident.

Listening

A. Listening for the Main Idea. **Audio** Listen to the radio program. As you listen, try to answer this question:

• According to Ronald Siegel, why is it "normal" to feel some paranoia?

B. Guessing Meaning from Context. **Audio** Listen to parts of the program. This time, listen for explanations of the following terms. Then write in your own words what you think the terms mean.

1. streptococcus A infection = _____

_____

2. premonitions = _____

_____

C. Listening for Details. **Audio** Listen to the program again. This time, listen for details that answer these questions.

1. Why can anyone become paranoid? _____

_____

2. Why did some people call the 1990s "The Age of Paranoia"? _____

_____

3. What percent of hospital admissions are for paranoia? _____

4. Is there a treatment for paranoia? _____

After Listening

A. Comprehension Check. **Pair** Answer these questions.

1. Why is it "normal" to feel some paranoia?

2. Why was there an increase in the cases of paranoia in the 1990s?

3. Why is paranoia so difficult to treat?

B. Discussion. Group   Discuss the answers to these questions.

1. Can you think of any other famous people in history who may have suffered from paranoia?

2. Many people enjoy experiencing fear in a safe way, such as by reading about or watching extremely frightening situations. Can you think of any popular TV shows or movies that provide this experience? Why do people like these kinds of movies and programs? Do you like them? Why or why not?

. : : : : : **Part Five** Academic English: Anxiety Disorders

Before Listening

A. Discussion. Group   You are going to listen to a lecture about **anxiety disorders.** An anxiety disorder is a mental illness that results when worry or fear becomes so extreme that a person cannot function normally. Before you listen, discuss the answers to these questions.

1. Most people feel anxious from time to time. What kinds of things make people feel anxious? Have you ever felt anxious?

2. What are some of the effects of feeling extremely anxious? In other words, can it affect your health? What other aspects of your life can it affect?

3. If you had a friend who felt anxious, what would you suggest that he or she do in order to feel less anxious?

B. Predicting. Pair   In the lecture, you will hear about different types of anxiety disorders and about treatments for anxiety disorders. What do you think some treatments for anxiety might be? Make predictions.

C. Thinking Ahead.   Look at the note-taking chart for the lecture on page 203 or the outline on pages 204–208 and think about your discussion in Exercise A. What would you like to know about anxiety disorders? Write two or three questions about the subject.

_____

_____

_____

D. Guessing Meaning from Context. In the lecture, you are going to hear some words that may be new to you. Before you listen, guess the meaning of some of the words from the lecture. The words are underlined in the sentences. Look for clues to their meaning in the words around them.

Write your guess in the blank after each sentence. Then check your guess with your teacher or the dictionary.

1. If you feel so much <u>apprehension</u> about flying, I suggest that you see a therapist and try to find out what is worrying you.

   Guess: _____

2. That student is so <u>preoccupied</u> by his mother's illness that he is having trouble paying attention in class.

   Guess: _____

3. Some of the <u>physiological</u> problems that result from anxiety are muscle tenseness and skin irritations.

   Guess: _____

4. Some therapists say that you must <u>confront</u> your fears because if you face them, you can get rid of them.

   Guess: _____

5. The therapist had Harrison climb slightly higher steps on each visit, and gradually his fear of heights <u>diminished</u>.

   Guess: _____

6. He stopped taking the drug for his anxiety disorder because of the <u>side effects</u>. When he took the pills, he was sleepy all the time.

   Guess: _____

7. The most disturbing symptom that Emily's anxiety disorder caused was <u>withdrawal</u>—she refused to speak to anyone for days.

   Guess: _____

E. Vocabulary Preparation: Idioms and Phrasal Verbs.   The speaker uses some idiomatic expressions and phrasal verbs in the lecture. First, read each sentence and guess the meaning of the underlined words. Then choose their meaning from the definitions in the box. Write the letter in the blanks.

Definitions

a. give your opinion   *c.* any thought he thinks of

b. handle, deal with   *d.* forget about it

Sentences

_____ **1.** This problem has gotten so big that I can't <u>cope with</u> it any more—I need help.

_____ **2.** If you don't agree, you should <u>speak up</u>.

_____ **3.** I just can't <u>get</u> that song <u>out of my mind</u>; I keep hearing it over and over!

_____ **4.** He doesn't think about what he says; he just says <u>whatever comes to mind</u>.

Listening

A. Listening for Main Ideas.   **Audio**   Listen to the lecture one time. Don't take notes. Don't worry about understanding everything. Just listen for the main idea. As you listen, try to answer these questions:

- What are some types of anxiety disorders?

- What are some treatments for anxiety disorders?

listening Strategy

Using Greek Roots to Guess Meaning   **Audio**

One way to guess meaning from context is by using your knowledge of word roots. Many medical and psychological terms come from Greek and Latin. Psychological researchers have combined a variety of Greek roots with "phobia" to name particular fears. For example, *acrophobia* comes from the Greek words for "high or extreme" and "fear." It means "fear of heights." The names for other psychological conditions use Greek roots, too. Take a look at the list on the next page of roots and affixes derived from Greek and their meanings:

Greek Roots	Meanings
acro-	a high place
agora-	the market place; an open, crowded place
arachno-	spider
claustro-	a closed place
hydro-	water
photo-	light
psycho-	the mind
-tropic	affecting; turning towards
xeno-	foreign /'zi no/

B. Vocabulary Practice. (Audio)   Practice using some Greek roots to name problems. Listen to and read the situations and answer the questions.

Situation 1. Molly is afraid of spiders. What problem does she have?

_____

Situation 2. Jack is uncomfortable in bright light. What's his problem?

_____

Situation 3. June doesn't like foreigners. What's her problem?

_____

Situation 4. Morgan is afraid of water. What problem does he have?

_____

C. Using Greek Roots to Guess Meaning from Context. (Audio)   Listen to parts of the lecture. This time, use your knowledge of Greek roots to guess the meaning of each of the following terms. Then write in your own words what you think the term means.

1. acrophobia = _____

2. claustrophobia = _____

3. psychotropic drugs = _____

listening **Strategy**

Listening to Lecture Introductions   Audio

The introduction to a lecture often contains a lot of important information. It can do any or all of the following:

- explain or define the topic
- define important terms
- present the structure of the rest of the lecture

All of these help you prepare for taking notes, so listen carefully to the introduction when a lecture begins.

D. Listening to a Lecture Introduction.   Audio   Listen to the introduction to the lecture. Listen for information that answers these questions.

1. How is anxiety defined?

_____

2. What are some examples of the kinds of anxiety that we all experience as part of our daily lives?

_____

_____

3. What are some ways we cope with anxiety?

_____

_____

4. What do we call anxiety that is frequent, persistent, painful, and unpleasant?

_____

5. What are three common anxiety disorders?

_____

_____

listening Strategy

Using a Chart to Take Notes Audio

One way to take lecture notes is to make a chart and fill it in as you listen. Sometimes you can use a chart alone to take notes; other times, you will need a chart in addition to a traditional outline. This works especially well for lecture topics that naturally suggest some sort of categorization. Examples are lectures that present types or kinds of things and comparisons of things. It also helps if you know the major categories of information that the lecture will cover *before* you hear it so you can draw the chart before the lecture begins. Sometimes the title of the lecture will give you the major categories covered in the lecture. Here are some examples of lecture topics and the charts that they suggest:

• Types of Phobias

Types of Phobias

Name	Definition	Example
claustrophobia	fear of enclosed places	fear of riding in elevators

• Types and Treatments of Abnormal Behavior

Types of Abnormal Behavior

Name	Definition	Example
schizophrenia	loss of contact with reality	hearing voices that aren't there

Treatments for Abnormal Behavior

Name	Definition	Example
psychotropic drugs	drugs that affect the brain	Benzodiazepines (tranquilizers)

• A Comparison of Western and Non-Western Psychological Disorders

Disorder	Definition	Western Example	Non-Western Example
Anorexia nervosa	Obsession with weight; refusal to eat	United States and Europe	Not found in Asia

E. Taking Notes: Using a Chart. (Audio)   Listen to the lecture again. This time take notes using the chart. Write down as much information as you can in each category.

Types of Anxiety Disorders

Name	Definition	Example

Treatments for Anxiety Disorders

Name	Definition	Example

F. Taking Notes: Using an Outline. (Audio)   Listen to the lecture again. This time fill in a traditional outline. Write your notes in the blanks.

Anxiety Disorders: Types and Treatments

I. Characteristics of Anxiety

   A. Definition: _____ *an emotional state of fear, apprehension or worry*

   _*that affects many areas of functioning*_____

     1. Affects _____

     2. Patient might not know _____

B. Part of our daily experiences. Examples:

1. _____

2. _____

3. _____

C. Ways to cope with anxiety

1. Test: _____

2. Staying healthy: _____

D. "Normal" anxiety becomes an anxiety disorder when _____

_____

II. Types of Anxiety Disorders

A. Generalized anxiety disorder

1. Persons continually tense with excessive worry about 2 or more life problems such as

a. _____

b. _____

c. _____

d. _____

2. Develops physical symptoms such as

a. _____

b. _____

c. _____

d. _____

e. _____

B. Phobic disorder

1. Definition: _____

_____

2. Causes _____

_____

3. Two types of phobic disorder:

   a. _____

      Examples:

       1) _____

       2) _____

       3) _____

   b. _____

      Examples:

       1) _____

       2) _____

       3) _____

C. Obsessive-compulsive disorder

  1. Definition of obsessions: _____

    _____

    Examples:

     a. _____

     b. _____

  2. Definition of compulsions: _____

    _____

    Examples:

     a. _____

     b. _____

III. Treatments for Anxiety Disorders

A. Psychodynamic therapy

  1. Definition: _____

    _____

  2. How it works: _____

    _____

  3. Two basic techniques:

     a. _____

     b. _____

B. Behavioral therapy

  1. Definition: _____

    _____

  2. Used in the treatment of _____

  3. Three major behavioral techniques:

    a. _____

      1) Phobic patient learns to _____

        _____

      2) Three phases of systematic desensitization:

        a) _____

        b) _____

        c) _____

    b. _____

      1) Exposed to _____ many times

      2) Patients made to realize _____

      Examples:

      a) Claustrophobic: _____

        _____

      b) Obsessive-compulsive: _____

        _____

    c. _____

      1) Form of learning in which _____

        _____

      2) Confronts feared object while _____

      Examples:

      a) _____

        _____

      b) _____

        _____

C. Drug therapies

   1. Psychotropic drugs

      a. Definition: _____

      b. Kinds of psychotropic drugs:

         1) Anti-anxiety drugs: minor tranquilizers that _____

            _____

         2) Most popular group of anti-anxiety drugs are _____

            _____ :

            a) _____

            b) _____

            c) _____

         3) Anti-psychotic; help relieve

            a) Confused thinking

            b) Withdrawal

            c) Generalized anxiety disorder

   2. Drugs, if overused, may cause _____

Source: Adapted from a lecture written by Paulette V. Starling, Ph.D., and Grace G. Cukras, Ph.D. Copyright © 2000 by McGraw-Hill. All rights reserved.

After Listening

A. Discussion. Pair   Discuss the answers to these questions.

1. Which note-taking method worked best for you, filling in a chart or using a traditional outline? Why?

2. Could you combine the two methods? How?

B. Using Your Notes. Group   Use your notes to discuss these questions about the lecture.

1. When does normal anxiety become an anxiety disorder?

2. What are some types of anxiety disorders?

3. What are the ways of treating anxiety disorders? How does each one work?

4. Do you ever experience "normal" anxiety? What do you do to cope with it?

Step Beyond

A. Doing Research. `Group`   You are going to do research on a topic related to anxiety disorders, paranoia, or another aspect of abnormal behavior that interests you. You will then present your topic to the class in a panel discussion. (In a panel discussion, three or more people present their ideas on different aspects of the same topic.)

First, form small groups. In your groups, pick a question from this list that interests you:

- What are the ways of treating anxiety disorders?

- Are there cultural differences in treating anxiety disorders?

- Who is more likely to have a phobia, a woman or a man?

- Who is more likely to have an anxiety disorder, a man or a woman?

- Are there phobias that exist in some cultures but not in others?

- Does paranoia exist in all cultures?

- Are there cultural differences in the way people define abnormal behavior?

- How successful are treatments for paranoia?

- Your question: _____

  _____

Now do your research on your own. Do Web or library research, or find an introductory psychology textbook. Answer your question, and find at least three examples that support your answer. You are going to present your information from your notes (see Chapter Four, page 143), so as you do your research, take notes on index cards, or use a form like the following.

Your question:
_____
Your answer:
_____
Example 1:
_____
_____
(Continued)

Example 2:
_____

_____

Example 3:
_____

_____

More examples:
_____

_____

Additional notes:
_____

_____

_____

 academic **Strategy**

Paraphrasing

In academic discussions, you sometimes need to paraphrase—explain in your own words—the ideas of experts. One way to do this is to take notes using synonyms as you do research, so you begin paraphrasing right away. Synonyms are words or phrases that mean about the same thing as the original.

Here is an example of paraphrasing:

In an article on kinds of treatment for anxiety disorders, you read the following:

> Modeling is a form of learning in which a patient acquires responses by observing and imitating others. In this treatment, the therapist is the one who confronts the feared object while the fearful patient watches.

In a class discussion, you might say the following:

> A patient can learn new responses by modeling—that is, watching and imitating another person. So, in this type of treatment, a patient can watch the therapist face the object that the patient is afraid of. Then the patient can learn to imitate the therapist who successfully copes with the feared object.

Notice that the paraphrase

✓ can be longer than the original statement

✓ means exactly the same thing as the original statement

✓ contains a few words that have not been changed—it's OK not to paraphrase specialized words, such as "psychotropic drugs"

Practice.   Practice paraphrasing the following statements about anxiety disorders.

1. A generalized anxiety disorder develops when a person is continually tense with excessive or severe worry about two or more life problems.

   _____

   _____

   _____

2. Obsessions are unwanted, disturbing, and unreasonable thoughts or ideas that people can not get out of their minds. An obsession can involve a disturbing concern with dirt and germs or a concern that something terrible might happen.

   _____

   _____

   _____

   _____

3. However, if these drugs are overused or misused, they can cause physical dependency and mild to severe side effects. Also these drugs do not provide a permanent solution for most cases of anxiety.

   _____

   _____

   _____

B. Participating in a Panel Discussion.   Now present your information from Exercise A in a panel discussion. To start, get together with the people who chose the same question as you. Go over your notes and organize your information. Your discussion will be more interesting if you each present a different answer to the question, or different examples that support the answer. Then decide as a class on the time limit for each panel, or each speaker on the panel.

  Panel discussions usually have a moderator—a person who watches the time and makes transitions from one speaker to the next. The moderator can be your teacher, or another student.

  Now have each panel present its information. Be sure to

✓ paraphrase information from your research

✓ use your notes; don't read

✓ make eye contact with the audience

✓ stay within the time limit

✓ take and answer questions from the audience when you are finished

speaking **Strategy**

Asking Questions after a Presentation

It's a good idea to ask the speaker a question after the presentation. Sometimes you'll have a question in mind before the presentation begins; other times, you'll think of one while you are listening. Keep a piece of paper nearby while you are listening to write down your question so you won't forget it when the time for questions comes. Asking questions after a presentation not only increases your knowledge on a subject, it also helps you pay attention and shows the speaker that you are interested in the subject.

C. Evaluating a Presentation.   **Group**   In small groups (different from your own panel group), evaluate the panel discussions. Use the following questions in your evaluation.

✓ Were the presentations easy to understand?

✓ Were the topics interesting?

✓ Did the speakers use notes and make good eye contact?

✓ Did the speakers present their points with appropriate examples?

✓ Did the speakers get interesting questions after their presentations? Did they give useful answers?

unit

4

Health:
Medicine
and Drugs

Addictive Substances

In this chapter, you'll listen to information about tobacco and other addictive substances. You'll also discuss smoking habits and whether certain addictive substances should be legal or not.

Part One Introduction: Addictive Substances on Campus

A. Brainstorming. **Group**   You are going to read an article about the use of addictive substances on college campuses in the United States. Before you read, list as many addictive substances as you can in your group. When you finish, indicate which you think are legal and which are illegal. For the legal substances, indicate the age you think you must be to use them. Write your answers in the chart.

Addictive Substances	Legal?	Illegal?	Age?

B. Predicting.   Look again at the list of addictive substances you made in Exercise A and make a prediction: Which of these substances do you think students use the most frequently on college campuses in the United States?

C. Thinking Ahead. (Pair)   Before you read, discuss the answers to these questions.

1. Have you noticed students using and/or selling addictive substances at your school? Which ones are the most common?

2. What problems can addictive substances cause for the people who use them? What problems can addictive substances cause for college students who use them?

D. Reading.   Read the following passage about the use of alcohol, tobacco, and other drugs on college campuses. As you read, try to answer this question:

• How do alcohol and other drugs affect students' performance in college?

Alcohol, Tobacco, and Other Drugs and the College Experience

In an interview with *TIME Magazine,* then University of Wisconsin Chancellor Donna Shalala was asked to identify the biggest problem on her campus. The answer was "alcohol." Despite the fact that the purchase of alcohol is illegal for most college students, alcohol is the most widely used drug on campus, with 41 percent of college students
5   reporting binge drinking—consuming five or more drinks in a row—at least once in the prior 2-week period.

After alcohol, tobacco and marijuana are the most frequently used drugs on campus. And the past few years have seen an increase in the use of LSD among college students.

Alcohol, tobacco, and other drug use have been linked to an array of negative con-
10 sequences that hurt students and jeopardize their futures.

• Almost one-third of the students at four-year institutions report missing class due to alcohol or other drug use.

• Nearly one-quarter of students report performing poorly on a test or project due to alcohol or other drug use.

15 • College students who drink the most obtain the lowest grades. A 1991 study found that while "A" students averaged 3.6 drinks per week and "B" students 5.5 drinks, "C" students averaged 7.6 drinks per week while "D" or "F" students averaged 10.6.

- According to a 1991 national survey of college students, the following
20   consequences resulted from drinking or drug use experienced at least once in the
past year: 63 percent had a hangover; 49.9 percent became nauseated or vomited;
39.3 percent regretted their actions; 36 percent drove while intoxicated; 33.2
percent got into an argument or fight; and 28 percent experienced memory loss.

These alcohol- and other drug-related incidents are costly, both in terms of dollars
25 and human potential. For instance, each year members of sororities and fraternities spend
roughly $200 million more on alcohol than all other students combined. That's enough to
cover the tuition, room, and board for tens of thousands of students. And student expen-
ditures for alcohol far exceed the operating costs for running college libraries.

The human cost is more difficult to quantify, but some facts are clear. About 159,000
30 of today's freshmen will drop out of college each year due to alcohol- and other drug-
related causes. Approximately 300,000 of today's students will eventually die of these
causes. Alcohol and other drugs also will be factors in thousands of incidents of unplanned
pregnancies, sexually transmitted diseases, including HIV/AIDS, and other consequences.

Source: Adapted from *Alcohol, Tobacco, and Other Drugs and the College Experience*. The National Clearinghouse for Alcohol and Drug Information,1995. <http://www.health.org/pubs/makelink/ml-collg.htm>

E. Discussion. Group Discuss the answers to these questions.

1. Was the prediction that you made in Exercise B correct? Were you surprised by any of the information in the article?

2. Is alcohol, tobacco, and/or marijuana use a problem at your school?

3. If there is a problem with alcohol, tobacco, and/or marijuana use at a school or college, what is a possible solution? Do you think that the solution should be the same for all three substances?

4. Even though alcohol and tobacco are legal, do you think they should be **banned** (not allowed) on college campuses? Why or why not?

5. Discuss addiction. What is it? What are some things that people become addicted to? How do people become addicted to substances? What are some treatments for addiction? Is it possible to smoke, drink alcohol, or take illegal drugs in **moderation** (in reasonable amounts) and not become addicted?

6. In your opinion, should illegal addictive substances such as cocaine and heroin be legalized? Why or why not?

F. Response Writing.   Choose *one* of these topics. Write about it for ten minutes. Don't worry about grammar and don't use a dictionary. Just put as many ideas as you can on paper.

- Should alcohol and/or tobacco be banned on college campuses? Why or why not?

- Should addictive drugs such as cocaine and heroin become legal or remain illegal? Explain your answer.

- Should marijuana be legalized?

- In your opinion, is it possible to try addictive substances and not become addicted?

Part Two   Everyday English: Secondhand Smoke

Before Listening

A. Thinking Ahead.   **Pair**   You are going to listen to Jennifer, Victor, and Brandon complain about people smoking. Before you listen, discuss the answers to these questions.

1. Do you smoke? If so, do other people complain about it? If you don't, what do you think about people who smoke?

2. Should smokers have the right to smoke wherever they want? Why or why not?

3. Is secondhand smoke a health problem? (**Secondhand smoke** means smoke that comes from another person who is smoking nearby.)

B. Predicting.   **Group**   The students give some ideas for why people smoke. What do you think they will say? Discuss and then write your predictions.

_____

_____

_____

_____

C. Vocabulary Preparation.
In the conversation, the students use some words and expressions that may be new to you. First, read each sentence and guess the meaning of the underlined words. Then choose their meaning from the definitions in the box. Write the letter in the blanks.

Sentences

_____ 1. David saw his neighbor die of a heart attack right in front of the building. He was shocked because it was the first time he'd ever seen a <u>corpse</u>.

_____ 2. She <u>smokes like a chimney</u>—one cigarette after another!

_____ 3. I don't <u>get</u> why they do that—it just doesn't make any sense to me!

_____ 4. I exercise <u>to keep</u> my weight <u>down</u>.

_____ 5. I can't exercise just before a meal—it <u>kills</u> my appetite.

_____ 6. Those <u>billboards</u> along Highway 101 with the enormous advertisements for cigarettes are ugly.

_____ 7. When you see how silly some kids look when they smoke, it makes you <u>think twice</u> about starting the habit.

_____ 8. I was going to go to the library, but the weather is so nice, I think I'll <u>hang around</u> outside for a while.

_____ 9. My grandfather had <u>Alzheimer's disease</u>. It caused him to lose his short-term memory, and after a while, he didn't even recognize me.

_____ 10. Many people complain about the tobacco company that uses a cartoon character in its ads because they believe that the ads <u>target</u> kids.

Definitions

a. understand

b. remain

c. consider carefully

d. smokes a lot

e. a disease that affects the brain

f. large signs displayed along highways that advertise products

g. to maintain a low level

h. removes, gets rid of

i. aim at, appeal to

j. dead body

Listening

A. Listening for Main Ideas. `Video/Audio` Now listen to the conversation. As you listen, try to answer these questions:

- Why do some people smoke?

- How do they start smoking?

B. Listening for Supporting Information. `Video/Audio` Listen to the conversation. This time, listen for information that supports the two main ideas: why some people smoke and how they start.

1. How does smoking keep a person's weight down?

Supporting idea 1: _____

_____

Supporting idea 2: _____

_____

2. What are two ways that young people might start smoking?

Supporting idea 1: _____

_____

Supporting idea 1: _____

_____

listening **Strategy**

Understanding Sarcasm `Audio`

People sometimes use sarcasm to be funny when they speak. Sarcasm is using words that are the opposite of what the speaker actually means. That's why it can be difficult even for native speakers to catch. You can sometimes recognize sarcasm by the person's intonation pattern. Listen to these "real" opinions followed by sarcastic remarks. Can you hear the difference?

Here are some examples:

- That Professor Taylor is a real smart guy. [Real opinion.]
- That Professor Taylor is a real smart guy. [Sarcastic remark.]

- Hey, smoking sounds like a great way to avoid Alzheimer's! [Real opinion.]
- Hey, smoking sounds like a great way to avoid Alzheimer's! [Sarcastic remark.]

C. Understanding Sarcasm. Video/Audio   Listen again to some parts of the conversation. Then circle *yes* or *no* to answer the questions.

1. Does Brandon think smoking is a good idea?	Yes	No
2. Does Victor think smoking is a good idea?	Yes	No
3. Does Jennifer think being near secondhand smoke is a good idea?	Yes	No
4. Does Victor think being near secondhand smoke is a good idea?	Yes	No

D. Listening for Details. Video/Audio   Listen to parts of the conversation again. Listen for details that answer these questions.

1. Does Jennifer think it is unusual to see people smoking?

_____

_____

2. The students discuss two effects of smoking. What are they?

_____

_____

3. The students imply that one effect is possibly positive and one is negative. Which is positive? Which is negative?

Possible positive effect: _____

Negative effect: _____

After Listening

A. Taking a Survey. Group   You are going to interview three students in your class about their opinions about smoking.

Step One

Make predictions about the results of your survey. Discuss the answers to these questions.

1. Do you think most people in your class *do* or *do not* smoke?

2. Do age, sex, and/or culture have anything to do with smoking habits?

Step Two

Now survey three students. If possible, try to talk to both males and females from different cultures and of different age groups. Write their answers in the chart. (If you don't want to give your age, simply avoid answering the question.) Write your own question.

Student	Student 1	Student 2	Student 3
Name	_____	_____	_____
Sex	☐ Male ☐ Female	☐ Male ☐ Female	☐ Male ☐ Female
Part 1			
1. Do you smoke now?	☐ Yes ☐ No	☐ Yes ☐ No	☐ Yes ☐ No
2. Have you ever smoked?	☐ Yes ☐ No	☐ Yes ☐ No	☐ Yes ☐ No
3. How old are you?			
4. Where did you grow up?			
Part 2			
5a. If you don't smoke, why don't you? **5b.** If you do smoke, why do you?			
6a. If you don't smoke, do smokers bother you? How or why? **6b.** If you smoked in the past, or if you smoke now, do you think that you bother people? How or why?			
7. Write your own question here. _____ _____ _____ _____			

B. Discussing Survey Results. Group   Form small groups. Try not to be in a group with some-one that you interviewed. Discuss the results of your survey. Now that you have your results, use them to answer again the questions you discussed in Step One and some additional questions.

1. Do most people in your class smoke?

2. Do age, sex, and/or culture have anything to do with smoking habits?

3. What are some reasons for smoking among the smokers in your class? (Question 5.)

4. Do age, sex, and/or culture have anything to do with reasons for smoking?

5. Do age, sex, and/or culture have anything to do with tolerating smoking and smokers? (Question 6.)

6. What other information about smoking and smokers surprised or interested you?

. : : : : :   Part Three   The Mechanics of Listening and Speaking

Language Functions

Agreeing Audio

There are several ways to express agreement with someone else's ideas in a conversation. Here are some examples:

A: . . . and then there's all the advertising, especially billboards . . .

B: Yeah.   **Less Formal**

   Yeah. I agree.

   Well, you're right.

   You've got a good point.

   Yes, I know what you mean.   **More Formal**

Disagreeing Audio

There are also several ways to express disagreement with someone's ideas in a conversation. Here are some examples:

A: Advertising makes young people want to smoke.

B: I don't think so.   **Less Formal**

I don't know.

I'm not so sure.

I disagree.

I disagree with you.   **More Formal**

A. Practice. Audio

Listen to some speakers give their opinions. If you agree, answer with one of the agreement expressions in the box on page 224. If you disagree, answer with one of the disagreement expressions in the box above.

Examples: A: People who smoke in public are a danger to others.

B: I disagree with you.

A: People who smoke in public are a danger to others.

B: You've got a good point.

1. Agree or disagree? _____

2. Agree or disagree? _____

3. Agree or disagree? _____

4. Agree or disagree? _____

5. Agree or disagree? _____

6. Agree or disagree? _____

Language Function

Expressing Degrees of Agreement/Disagreement Audio

You can express degrees (weak, neutral, or strong) of agreement or disagreement. To do this, add one of the following words or expressions to your statement. Compare these examples:

Weak	Neutral	Strong
I <u>sort of</u> (dis)agree with you.	I (dis)agree with you.	I <u>really</u> (dis)agree with you.
I <u>kind of</u> (dis)agree with you.		I <u>totally</u> (dis)agree with you.
I don't <u>really</u> agree with that.		I <u>completely</u> (dis)agree with you.
<u>I'm not sure</u> I agree with that.		I (dis)agree <u>a hundred percent</u>!
<u>I don't know</u> if I agree.		

B. Practice. Audio   Listen to these statements of agreement and disagreement. Decide if they are weak, neutral, or strong. Check (✓) the correct answer.

Statement	Weak	Neutral	Strong
1			
2			
3			
4			
5			
6			

C. Practice. Audio   Practice expressing degrees of agreement. Respond to each statement according to your own opinion, but express the degree indicated by the cue.

1. (Strong) _____

2. (Neutral) _____

3. (Weak) _____

4. (Weak)   _____

5. (Neutral) _____

6. (Strong) _____

7. (Strong) _____

8. (Strong) _____

Language Function

Expressing an Opinion Audio

People rarely agree or disagree without expressing an opinion as well. If you agree, your opinion might include the following:

- a restatement of the other person's idea
- an extension of the idea
- an additional idea that supports the same point

If you disagree, your opinion might include the following:

- the opposite of the other person's idea
- an explanation of why you disagree

Since your opinion follows your agreement or disagreement statement, certain expressions help make this transition. You saw some of these in Chapter Three, page 95.

Here are some more examples:

A: Advertising makes young people want to smoke.

B: Oh, I don't know. I think kids are smarter than that.

A: Advertising makes young people want to smoke.

B: I agree. In my opinion, advertising is the main reason kids start smoking.

D. Practice. Audio   Practice agreeing or disagreeing and expressing an opinion. Listen again to the statements you heard in Exercise A. This time, agree or disagree, and give your opinion.

Pronunciation

Reduced Forms: *a* and *of* Audio

When people speak quickly, some words become reduced, or short. Here are some examples.

Long Form	**Short Form**
What a choice!	Whatta* choice!
Get a drink for me, OK?	Getta* drink for me, OK?
Want a snack?	Wanna snack?
Let's get out of here!	Let's get outta* here!
A couple of my friends smoke.	A coupla my friends smoke.
Some of them smoke.	Somma them smoke.
I kind of disagree.	I kinda disagree.
I sort of disagree.	I sorta disagree.

*Note: The *t* sound in "whatta," "getta," and "outta" sounds more like a *d*.

E. Practice. Audio   People say the short forms but write the long forms. Listen to the conversation and write the long form of the words you hear.

A: A _____ _____ my friends and I are going to that new pizza place.
                  1

B: _____ _____ my friends went there last week. They have 20 _____ _____
              2   3

pizza. _____ _____ choice!
                      4

A: _____ _____ snack? I can _____ _____ pizza for you . . .
              5   6

B: Uhmm, I think I'll go with you guys . . .

A: OK I'm hungry! Let's get _____ _____ here!
                                            7

Review: Language Functions

Agreeing Video/Audio

Listen to these examples of how to express agreement. You'll use this function in the next section.

Put It Together

A. Forming an Opinion.   You are going to agree or disagree with your partner about certain topics and add an opinion. Before you start, look at the following list of topics from this book and form an opinion about each one. Add your own topic if you like.

Topics

• Offering bribes to get business

Opinion: _____

_____

• Government assistance for the poor

Opinion: _____

_____

• Pop Art

  Opinion: _____

  _____

• The importance of Greek art

  Opinion: _____

  _____

• The purpose of dreaming

  Opinion: _____

  _____

• What is "normal"

  Opinion: _____

  _____

• The legalization of drugs

  Opinion: _____

  _____

• Your topic _____

  Opinion: _____

  _____

B. Agreeing, Disagreeing, and Expressing an Opinion. **Pair** Now discuss your opinions. Take turns speaking first. Follow these directions:

1. Student A gives an opinion about one of the topics.

2. Student B will agree or disagree. Use the expressions in the boxes on pages 224–225. Express weak, neutral, or strong agreement or disagreement, depending on how you really feel. Use the expressions in the box on page 226. Then follow with an opinion statement.

3. Exchange roles.

...:::: **Part Four** Broadcast English: Smoking
                                    as a "Gateway" Drug

Before Listening

A. Thinking Ahead. **Group**   You are going to listen to a radio program about whether smoking is a **gateway** drug, a drug that makes the user want to take other drugs. Before you listen, discuss the answers to these questions.

1. The **premise** (underlying idea) of this program is that tobacco (or nicotine, one of the chemicals in tobacco) is a drug. Do you agree with this? In what way is it a drug?

2. Do you think that taking one drug can lead to taking more drugs? Why or why not?

B. Predicting. **Pair**   Before you listen, make a prediction about what you are going to hear. Discuss the answer to these questions.

• Do you think the program will say that smoking *is* or *is not* a gateway drug? Why?

C. Guessing Meaning from Context.

In the radio program, you are going to hear some words that may be new to you. Before you listen, guess the meaning of some of the words from the program. The words are underlined in the sentences. Look for clues to their meaning in the words around them.

Write your guess in the blank after each sentence. Then check your guess with your teacher or the dictionary.

1. Why do you <u>engage in</u> that kind of behavior? Don't you know that by doing those things, you are risking your health?

   Guess: _____

2. Some researchers <u>hypothesize</u> that tobacco is a gateway drug; they believe that smoking leads to other kinds of drug taking.

   Guess: _____

3. <u>Substance abuse</u> is a growing problem on college campuses. Studies show that students are drinking more alcohol and taking more drugs than ever before.

   Guess: _____

4. Many kids start smoking because they like the <u>notion</u> of taking a risk.

   Guess: _____

5. Lloyd Johnston believes that cigarette smoking is one of the <u>causal factors</u> of marijuana smoking. In his study, kids who smoke a pack of cigarettes a day are 26 times more likely to smoke marijuana than those who don't smoke cigarettes.

   Guess: _____

6. Greg was in prison for possessing marijuana, but now he's <u>on probation</u>. That means he's free, as long as he follows certain rules and meets regularly with his probation officer.

   Guess: _____

D. Vocabulary Preparation. The speakers use some idiomatic expressions in the radio program. First, read each sentence and guess the meaning of the underlined words. Then choose their meaning from the definitions in the box. Write the letter in the blanks.

> **Definitions**
>
> *a.* become addicted   *d.* a part of a process
>
> *b.* illegal   *e.* risking getting arrested
>
> *c.* serious enforcement of a law or policy

Sentences

_____ **1.** There's finally been a <u>crackdown</u> on going through red lights in San Francisco; the city has mounted cameras at major intersections to catch people who do it.

_____ **2.** Learning academic English is <u>a step along the way</u> to success in an American university.

_____ **3.** Some people think that if you are addicted to nicotine, you <u>get hooked on</u> illegal drugs such as heroin later on.

_____ **4.** A lot of kids start smoking before they start <u>illicit</u> drugs simply because cigarettes are easily available.

_____ **5.** If you have marijuana in your possession, you're <u>flirting with the law</u>, because it's illegal.

Listening

A. Listening for Main Ideas. **Audio** Listen to the radio program. As you listen, try to answer this question:

- The program presents two sides of the question: Is smoking a gateway drug? What are the two sides of the argument?

1. It *is* a gateway drug because _____

_____

2. It *isn't* a gateway drug because _____

_____

B. Listening for Two Sides of an Argument. Audio   Listen to part of the program again. Vicky
Quay interviews four researchers. Listen for information that answers these questions and complete the
chart.

1. Which of them believe that there is a direct connection between smoking and using illegal
   drugs? Which of them do not?

2. What reasons do they give for their beliefs?

Researcher	Direct Connection?	Why? (or: What *Is* the Cause)
Johnston	Yes	
Beals		
Yu		
Cleaver		

listening Strategy

Listening for Experts' Qualifications   Audio

It's important to pay attention to the qualifications of people who are expressing their opinions about
scientific or social scientific ideas. To effectively evaluate their opinions, you often need to know
this information:

- their job title

- their degrees

- their **affiliations** (the institutions they work for or represent)

- their research

For example, a biology professor at a well-known university might say that milk is good for you.
However, if the Milk Advisory Board pays her for consulting services, this affiliation might influence her opinions.

C. Listening for Experts' Qualifications. Audio

Listen to parts of the program. You will hear each expert's job title, qualifications, and/or affiliations. Match the job titles, qualifications, and affiliations with the experts. Write the letters of the qualifications that match in the blank next to each expert. (There may be more than one for each person.) Then answer the questions that follow.

Experts	Qualifications
_____ **1.** Lloyd Johnston	*a.* psychologist
_____ **2.** Howard Beals	*b.* University of Michigan
_____ **3.** Jian Yu	*c.* R. J. Reynolds Tobacco Company
_____ **4.** Herbert Cleaver	*d.* George Washington University
	e. sociologist
	f. Columbia University
	g. professor

Questions

1. Which expert has both a job title and a university affiliation? _____

2. Which expert does not have a university affiliation? _____

3. Which expert has an affiliation with a university and a company? _____

4. Which expert has an affiliation that might influence his opinions? _____

 academic Strategy

Understanding Latin Terms Audio

People often use Latin terms (and terms that come from Latin) in formal speaking situations. The more you hear them, the better you'll understand them. Once you are comfortable with them, using them in academic speaking situations can make you sound more fluent. Here are some common Latin terms:

Latin Terms	Meanings
modus operandi	way of doing something; method or procedure
per se	by itself, by himself or herself, by themselves
pro forma	made or done in a routine manner
quid pro quo	this for that: you do something for me, and I'll do something for you
verbatim	word for word; literally

Practice.   Listen to these sentences and fill in the blanks with the Latin term you hear.

1. The detective found many clues that the thief left behind. This helped him to figure out the thief's _____, which then helped him to solve the crime.

2. The company has a _____ agreement that all consultants must sign. The agreement doesn't take into consideration your individual circumstances.

3. He's not a bad kid _____. He just hangs around with the wrong kind of friends and they get him into trouble.

4. Instead of using notes, he read his report _____, so it was pretty boring.

5. "This is a _____ arrangement," the lawyer told the accountant. "I'll represent you in court if you advise me on how to pay fewer taxes next year."

D. Understanding Latin Terms.   Audio   Listen to a part of the program. The speaker uses a Latin term. Paraphrase the speaker's statement by translating the Latin term and completing this sentence.

What he's saying is that cigarette smoking _____

_____

After Listening

Discussion.   Group   Discuss the answers to these questions.

1. The program presents two sides of the question: Is smoking a gateway drug? What are the two sides of the argument? Which side of the argument do you agree with? Why?

2. Evaluate the experts who were interviewed in the program. Were they qualified to speak on this subject? Does anything about any of these experts make you question their authority or reliability?

3. Think of an advertisement for smoking and describe it to the group. Whom does it target? How does it make smoking look attractive?

4. Think of movies that portray smoking, drinking, or illegal drug use. Do movies often make using addictive substances look attractive or unattractive? Do you think young people are influenced by these movies?

·..::!!! **Part Five** Academic English: Nicotine Addiction

Before Listening

A. Discussion. Group
You are going to listen to a lecture about how people become addicted to nicotine. Before you listen, discuss the answers to these questions.

1. What are the health risks of cigarette smoking?

2. What do cigarettes contain that is bad for you?

3. What other tobacco products are bad for your health?

4. If you had a friend who was addicted to nicotine, would you try to help your friend stop smoking? If so, what would you do?

B. Predicting. Pair
The lecture contains statistics on smoking in the United States. Make a prediction. Has smoking declined or increased in the United States in the last thirty years?

C. Thinking Ahead.
Look at the outline for the lecture on pages 240–241 and think about your discussion in Exercise A. What would you like to know about tobacco addiction? Write two or three questions about the subject.

_____

_____

_____

D. Guessing Meaning from Context.
In the lecture, you are going to hear some words that may be new to you. Before you listen, guess the meaning of some of the words from the program. The words are underlined in the sentences. Look for clues to their meaning in the words around them.

Write your guess in the blank after each sentence. Then check your guess with your teacher or the dictionary.

1. I <u>crave</u> chocolate. My desire for it is so strong that I can't stop eating it.

   Guess: _____

2. Jennifer, Victor, and Brandon were exposed to <u>passive smoke</u>; that's almost as bad for you as smoking itself.

   Guess: _____

3. Many people smoke because it gives them a feeling of <u>alertness</u>; this helps them pay attention and stay awake while they work.

   Guess: _____

4. You can have a <u>psychological dependence</u> on a drug if it has positive effects on your behavior and attitude.

   Guess: _____

5. Morgan wanted to stop smoking, but he was afraid that the <u>withdrawal</u> from cigarettes would make him feel bad.

   Guess: _____

6. When he stopped smoking, Morgan had feelings of <u>restlessness</u>—he couldn't relax.

   Guess: _____

7. Smoking is a health <u>hazard</u>. It's dangerous because it causes many serious diseases.

   Guess: _____

8. Mandy started smoking <u>casually</u>—just one or two cigarettes every once in a while—but soon she became addicted.

   Guess: _____

9. Jack wanted to stop smoking, but he wasn't able to control his behavior—he just didn't have the <u>willpower</u>.

   Guess: _____

10. Clara stopped smoking in 1995. She's been <u>smoke-free</u> for a long time now.

   Guess: _____

Listening

A. Listening for the Main Idea. Audio   Listen to the lecture one time. Don't take notes. Don't worry about understanding everything. Just listen for the main idea. As you listen, try to answer this question:

- Why is smoking addictive?

listening Strategy

Number Shortcuts (Audio)

When you hear numbers, you can write them using numerals or words. Sometimes it's faster to write the numeral. Other times, it's faster to write the word. In some cases, there's a shortcut—an abbreviation—for the number, and that might be the easiest to write. Choose the method that works best for you. Look at these examples:

Words	Numerals	Abbreviations
one million; a million	1,000,000	1 mill; 1 m
one thousand	1,000	1 k
forty thousand	40,000	40 k
sixty percent	60%	same as numeral: 60%
six to eight	6 to 8; 6–8	same as numeral: 6–8

B. Listening for Numerical Information. (Audio)   Listen to parts of the lecture. This time, listen for numerical information—numbers, percents, and quantities—about smoking. Fill in the blanks with the numbers you hear. Use words, numerals, or abbreviations.

Parts 1–3

_____ of people throughout the world smoke cigarettes. Despite the fact that cigarette
     ₁

smoking has declined in the United States over the past _____ years, there are still over
     ₂

_____ Americans who smoke.
     ₃

Parts 4–5

Let's take a look at the health risks of smoking. Smoking cigarettes *is* dangerous. In fact, it's the leading

cause of preventable death in the United States. Every year over _____ Americans die as a
     ₄

result of cigarette smoking, and another _____ people suffer from smoking-related diseases.
     ₅

Part 6

The symptoms of nicotine withdrawal can appear within _____ hours after the last cigarette
     ₆

is smoked.

Part 7

Of people who quit smoking, only about _____ remain smoke-free for more than one year.
     ₇

C. Taking Notes: Using an Outline. (Audio)   Listen to the lecture again. This time fill in the outline.

Nicotine Addiction

I. Introduction

   A. Cigarette smoking is _____

   B. Statistics on cigarette smoking

      1. In the U.S., smoking has _____

      2. Number who smoke: _____

      3. Higher rates among _____

   C. Health risks of cigarette smoking

      1. Number who die: _____

      2. Number who suffer from diseases: _____

      3. Smoking-related diseases and risks include _____

         _____

         _____

      4. Nonsmoking risks: _____

         _____

         _____

II. Why Smoking Is Addictive

   A. What causes young people to start? _____

     _____

     _____

   B. The addictive power of nicotine

      1. Cigarette smoke contains _____

         _____

      2. General effects of nicotine: _____

         _____

      3. Short-term effects: _____

         _____

4. Long-term effects: _____

_____

5. Psychological effects: _____

_____

6. Effects of nicotine withdrawal

   a. Symptoms include _____

_____

   b. Percent who remain smoke-free after one year: _____

_____

III. Strategies for Treating Nicotine Addiction

  A. Quitting on your own requires _____

  B. Other methods include

    1. _____

    2. _____

  C. Benefits of quitting smoking: _____

_____

Source: Adapted from a lecture written by Deborah E. Blocker, D. Sc., M. P. H., R. D., CDN. Copyright © 2000 by McGraw-Hill. All rights reserved.

Now listen again and complete the outline.

listening **Strategy**

Listening for Comparisons Audio

Sometimes statistical information includes comparisons of two groups. Words and expressions that signal comparisons such as these include the following:

- rates are greater/higher among X than Y
- rates are lower among X than Y

Other comparison expressions include the following:

• more than	• higher than	• more + (adjective) or (adverb)
• less than	• lower than	• less + (adjective) or (adverb)

D. Listening for Comparisons. (Audio)   Listen to part of the lecture. Listen for comparisons and answer the questions.

1. Who smokes more, men or women?

2. Who smokes more, whites or non-whites?

3. Who smokes more, people with a high school education, or people without a high school education?

After Listening

 speaking **Strategy**

The "Grammar" of Smoking

When you talk about starting, stopping, or trying smoking, you use some confusing combinations of main verb + a gerund or an infinitive. Verbs such as *stop, start,* * and *try* require either a gerund or an infinitive depending on what you want to say. Compare these sentences with *stop:*

• She <u>stopped smoking</u>. (She doesn't smoke anymore.)

• She <u>stopped to smoke</u>. (She stopped what she was doing so she could smoke a cigarette.)

Compare these sentences with *start* and *try:*

Sentences	Meanings
She <u>started smoking</u>.	She wasn't a smoker before, but now she is.
She <u>started to smoke</u>.	She started smoking. OR:
	She lit a cigarette and smoked it.
She <u>tried smoking</u>.	She never did it before; she experimented with it.
She <u>tried to smoke</u>.	She attempted it, but she failed.
She <u>tried stopping</u>.	She never did it before; she experimented with it.
She <u>tried to stop</u>.	She attempted it, but she failed.

*Note: After *start,* the gerund and the infinitive have about the same meaning.

Using Your Notes. (Group)   Use your notes to discuss these questions about the lecture.

1. How do people start smoking?

2. What are the health risks of cigarette smoking?

3. Why is smoking addictive?

4. What are some treatments for nicotine addiction?

5. What are the benefits of stopping smoking?

 Step Beyond

You are going to discuss a controversial issue in small groups. You are going to argue for or against one of the following issues:

- Alcohol (or tobacco products) should/shouldn't be banned on college campuses.
- Smoking should/shouldn't be illegal.
- Illegal drugs should/shouldn't be legalized.
- Smoking is/isn't a gateway drug.
- Marijuana should/shouldn't be legal.
- Marijuana/tobacco/another drug is/isn't addictive.
- It's possible/impossible to experiment with addictive substances and not become addicted.
- Your own controversial issue on the subject of addictive substances: _____

Step One

First, choose an issue that interests you. Decide on your position and do research.

Do Web or library research, or find information in an introductory health textbook. Find at least three reasons that support your argument. You are going to present your ideas from notes (see Chapter Four, page 143), so as you do your research, take notes on index cards, or use a form like the following:

Your issue:
_____
Thesis statement:
_____
Reason 1:
_____
_____
Reason 2:
_____
_____

(Continued)

Reason 3:

_____

_____

More reasons or other information:

_____

_____

_____

_____

Step Two

Go over your notes and organize your information.

Step Three

Form small groups. Decide on a time limit for each speaker. A good length is from three to five minutes. In your groups, present your issue. Follow these guidelines:

✓ paraphrase information from your research

✓ use your notes; don't read

✓ make eye contact with your group members

✓ stay within the time limit

✓ take and answer questions from your group members when you are finished

Step Four

After everyone has presented his or her issue, take some time to discuss the ones that interested you the most. Discuss each issue, using agreement and disagreement expressions and opinion statements.

Step Five

In your groups, evaluate each other's presentations. Use the following questions in your evaluation.

✓ Were the presentations easy to understand?

✓ Were the issues interesting?

✓ Did the speakers use notes and make good eye contact?

✓ Did the speakers support their thesis statements with good reasons?

chapter

Eight

Secrets of Good Health

In this chapter, you'll listen to information about health issues in different countries and discuss ways to maintain good health.

∴∴⋮⋮ **Part One** Introduction: Americans and Health

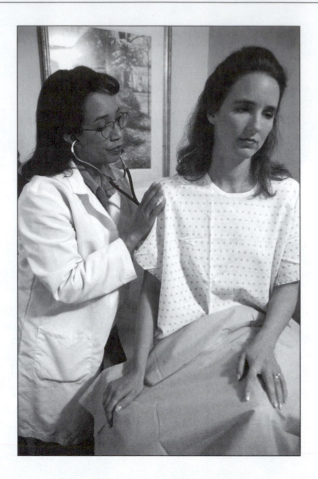

A. Discussion. **Pair**   You are going to read an article about how concerned Americans are with their health. Before you read, discuss the answers to these questions.

1. Are you concerned with your health? What do you do to stay healthy?

2. Is it important to see a doctor regularly, in your opinion?

3. Are alternative remedies such as herbal medicine and vitamins helpful in maintaining health or curing disease, in your opinion?

4. Do you think alternative therapies such as acupuncture are helpful in curing disease?

B. Predicting. Pair   The article gives some information about Americans and their concern with health. Make predictions about what you will read.

1. Are Americans generally healthy?

2. Do most see doctors frequently?

3. Are many Americans overweight?

4. Do they take a lot of prescription drugs?

5. Are they interested in alternative remedies and therapies?

C. Reading.   You are going to read about Americans' concern for their health. As you read, try to answer this question:

• Are Americans trying to live a healthier lifestyle than in the past?

Concern for Health Among Americans

Americans seem obsessed with taking care of their health, while at the same time, they admit that they aren't doing a very good job at it. Almost nine out of every ten Americans say that they have seen a doctor within the last three years, according to the latest *Wall Street Journal*/NBC News poll. Even most people without health insur-
5   ance reported that they had seen a doctor within three years.

"Health concerns cut across all social and economic divisions," says Thom Riehle, who helped conduct the poll.

In addition, many Americans say that taking care of their health is a daily habit. According to the same poll, half say that they take a prescription drug every day and women
10   from low-income backgrounds are more likely than most Americans to take prescription drugs.

Aside from regular visits, Americans are coming in contact with doctors in other ways. Almost two in five say that they have been to an emergency room in the past year, and one quarter say that they have had **elective** (not required) surgery in the past five years.
15   Despite such frequent trips to the doctor, many Americans are taking matters into their own hands. People are looking for health remedies outside of traditional medicine, with close to half saying either they or a family member have tried alternative remedies not prescribed by a doctor, such as herbs, vitamins, or special therapies.

Such numbers suggest that the doctor's word is no longer absolute. Sherry Hughes,
20   a 51-year-old arthritis sufferer from Kinston, North Carolina, has been taking glucosamine and chondroitin, amino acids that she obtained from her local health-food store, for the past nine months. While her physician-recommended pain pills simply "covered up" the problem, Hughes says that her natural remedies eliminated her hip pains and decreased the swelling in her hands and toes.

25   Still, despite this apparent careful attention to matters of personal health, problems persist. More than a third of respondents say they have a chronic or serious medical condition that will last for many years, and close to half say they are at least 15 pounds overweight.

"Many people are going to the doctor, but they're finding it hard to prevent the behav-
30 iors that put them at risk for long-term, chronic illness," says Dr. James Marks, director of the National Center for Chronic Disease Prevention and Health Promotion in Atlanta [Georgia], a division of the Centers for Disease Control and Prevention.

On a brighter side, adult smoking is leveling off. Only 26 percent of those 18 years and older say they smoke cigarettes or cigars regularly. That compares with 28.1 percent
35 ten years ago, according to the CDC, and is down from 34 percent twenty years ago and from 43 percent three decades ago.

Source: Kemba Dunham, adapted from "Concern for Health Cuts Across Social Boundaries" from *The Wall Street Journal* (June 25, 1998). Copyright © 1998 by Dow Jones and Company, Inc. Reprinted with the permission of *The Wall Street Journal*.

D. Discussion. [Group]   Discuss the answers to these questions.

1. Were the predictions that you made in Exercise B correct? Were you surprised by any of the information in the article?

2. Find details in the article that support the contrast statement at the beginning of the article: "Americans seem obsessed with taking care of their health, while at the same time, they admit that they aren't doing a very good job at it."

3. Compare American health practices and beliefs described in the article with those of your culture or another culture or country that you are familiar with. Compare the following:

    • concern with health

    • frequency of doctor visits

    • weight

    • smoking

    • use of prescription medicines

    • interest in alternative remedies and therapies

E. Response Writing.   Choose *one* of these topics. Write about it for ten minutes. Don't worry about grammar and don't use a dictionary. Just put as many ideas as you can on paper.

• Are you in good health, in your opinion? Why or why not?

• What is the secret to good health, in your opinion?

• Are there cultural differences in **approaches** (methods) to maintaining good health, in your opinion? Explain your answer.

∴∶∶∶∶∶ **Part Two** Everyday English: Tips for Good Health (Interview)

Before Listening

A. Thinking Ahead. (Group)   You are going to listen to Evan interview people on the street. He's going to ask them for their **tips** (advice) for good health. Before you listen, discuss the answers to these questions.

1. What's the difference between mental and physical health?

2. What's your definition of good physical health?

3. How do you define good mental health?

B. Predicting. (Group)   You are going to listen to people give their tips for good health. What do you think they will say? Discuss and then write your predictions.

_____

_____

_____

C. Vocabulary Preparation.   The students in the interview use some words and expressions that may be new to you. First, read each sentence and guess the meaning of the underlined word. Then choose their meaning from the definitions in the box. Write the letters in the blanks.

Sentences

_____ 1. Daniella <u>has a</u> very <u>positive image</u> about herself—she thinks she's smart and attractive.

_____ 2. If you think <u>healthy</u>, you'll be healthy.

_____ 3. He's got a <u>steady</u> job now, so he'll be able to save some money.

_____ 4. I think you fried those potatoes in too much cooking oil—they're sitting in a pool of <u>grease</u>.

_____ 5. If you continue to eat junk food, you'll <u>end up</u> sick and overweight.

_____ 6. <u>Eating right</u> is the key to staying healthy.

_____ 7. I'm really <u>stressed out</u>—my heart is pounding and I can't sleep at night.

_____ 8. The <u>key to</u> good health is exercising regularly.

Definitions

a. eating correctly

b. experiencing a lot of stress

c. has a good mental idea

d. vegetable or animal fat in food

e. become

f. think of yourself as being healthy

g. regular

h. most important part of

Listening

A. Listening for Main Ideas. [Video/Audio]   Now listen to the interview. As you listen, try to answer these questions:

- Do some speakers give advice for physical health?

- Do some give advice for mental health?

- Do some give advice for both?

B. Listening for Details. [Video/Audio]   Listen to the interview again. This time, fill in the chart below for each speaker.

- Does the speaker give advice for physical health, mental health, or both?

You'll listen to the interview two times. The first time you listen, just check (✔) the box(es) that apply. The second time, listen for the actual advice the speaker gives and write it in the correct space.

Speaker	Physical Health Tips?	Mental Health Tips?
1	✔ exercise, eat well	✔ have positive image, think healthy
2		
3		

(Continued)

Speaker	Physical Health Tips?	Mental Health Tips?
4		
5		
6		
7		
8		

listening **Strategy**

Guessing the Meaning of Proverbs from Context (Audio)

Every language has **proverbs**—well-known sayings that express some wisdom about life. If you hear a proverb that is new to you, you can sometimes guess its meaning from the context. Here is an example:

> Since the economy is bad and you already have a job, I don't think you should look for a new one right now. Remember, a bird in the hand is worth two in the bush.

You can guess that this proverb means that something you have right now is more valuable than something you might find later.

C. Guessing the Meaning of Proverbs from Context. (Video/Audio)   Listen to parts of the interview again. Guess the meaning of the following proverbs by paying attention to their contexts. Write your guesses in the blanks.

1. An apple a day keeps the doctor away = _____

_____

2. You are what you eat = _____

_____

D. Listening for Specific Information. (Video/Audio)   Listen again to some of the speakers' advice. Listen for answers to these questions.

1. Speaker 4: How many times a week should you exercise, according to this speaker?

   _____

   _____

2. Speaker 6: What are examples of getting "stressed out," according to this speaker?

   _____

   _____

3. Speaker 7: This speaker suggests specific activities for maintaining good health. What are they?

   _____

   _____

After Listening

A. Taking a Survey. (Group)   You are going to interview three students in your class about their tips for good health. Write their tips in the chart and write your own question.

Student Name _____	Student 1 _____	Student 2 _____	Student 3 _____
1. What is the key to good health, in your opinion?			
2. Write your own question about health here. _____ _____ _____			

B. Discussing Survey Results. Group   Form small groups. Try not to be in a group with someone that you interviewed. Discuss the results of your survey. Did any of the advice surprise you? Were
there any unusual suggestions?

. . : : : : : **Part Three** The Mechanics of Listening and Speaking

Language Function

Giving Advice Audio

There are several ways to give advice. Here are some examples:

You <u>ought to</u> get lots of rest.	**Less Formal**
You <u>should</u> get lots of rest.	
<u>It's a good idea</u> to get lots of rest.	
<u>I suggest that</u> you get lots of rest.	**More Formal**

A. Practice. (Audio)   Practice giving advice. Listen to the speaker and give the advice in the box below using one of the expressions on page 253.

Example: A: How can I improve my health?

B: You should avoid stress.

Expressions		
get lots of rest	avoid stress	have a positive image
eat healthy food	see your doctor once a year	follow an exercise program

Language Function

Degrees of Giving Advice   (Audio)

You can soften advice by adding "perhaps" or "I think." Here are some examples:

- <u>Perhaps</u> you should get more rest.
- <u>I think</u> you ought to get lots of rest.

You can also make advice stronger by adding words such as "really." Here is an example:

- You <u>really</u> ought to get more rest.

Sometimes people are very direct when they give advice. Here are some ways to be direct:

- Get lots of rest.
- Just get lots of rest.
- All you have to do is get lots of rest.

B. Practice. (Audio)   Listen to a speaker giving advice. Decide if the advice is soft, strong, or direct. Circle the correct answer.

1.	Soft	Strong	Direct		**4.**	Soft	Strong	Direct
2.	Soft	Strong	Direct		**5.**	Soft	Strong	Direct
3.	Soft	Strong	Direct					

C. Practice. (Audio)   Practice giving different degrees of advice. Listen to the speaker. Give the following advice. Give soft, strong, or direct advice, according to the cue.

Example: A: I don't feel well. What should I do?

B: (soft: get more rest) I think you should get more rest.

1. (soft: get more rest) _____

2. (strong: avoid stress) _____

3. (direct: eat better) _____

4. (soft: see your doctor) _____

5. (direct: follow an exercise program) _____

Pronunciation

/θ/* vs. /t/ (Audio)

It's important to hear the difference between these two sounds: /θ/ and /t/. Listen to these examples. Do you hear the difference?

/θ/	/t/
Do you know what he <u>th</u>ought?	Do you know what he <u>t</u>aught?

Now listen to these examples:

/θ/	/t/		/θ/	/t/
<u>th</u>ank	<u>t</u>ank		my<u>ths</u>	mi<u>tts</u>
<u>th</u>eme	<u>t</u>eam		ba<u>th</u>	ba<u>t</u>
<u>th</u>in	<u>t</u>in		pa<u>th</u>	pa<u>t</u>

*Note: The IPA (International Phonetic Symbol) for the voiceless *th* sound is /θ/.

D. Practice. (Audio)   In each pair of words, circle the one that you hear.

1. thank — tank

2. eighth — eight

3. thought — taught

4. tenth — tent

5. bath — bat

6. myths — mitts

7. thin — tin

8. thick — tick

9. fourth — fort

10. math — mat

11. theme — team

12. path — pat

E. Practice. `Pair`   Say one of the words from the Word List. (Don't say the words in order.) Your partner will write the word. Check each word to see if it matches. If your partner didn't write the correct word, try again. Then exchange roles.

Word List			
tank	eighth	eight	thought
tenth	bat	mitts	taught
tent	bath	myths	team
thin	tick	fort	pat
tin	thick	fourth	thank
math	mat	theme	path

listening Strategy

Using Context to Distinguish Sounds   `Audio`

You can use context to distinguish similar sounds. In other words, a word with a /θ/ sound usually won't have the same context as a similar word with a /t/ sound. Look at this sentence:

> The baseball <u>team</u> played well.

You know that you didn't hear the following sentence because it doesn't make sense:

> The baseball <u>theme</u> played well.

F. Practice. `Group`   Now use words with the /θ/ sound in conversations. Interview your classmates. Ask questions to fill in the chart or use the Word List above to make up your own. Write your classmates' names in the chart. Which student collects the most names?

Find someone who . . .	Names
has advice for maintaining good heal<u>th</u>	
brushes his/her tee<u>th</u> <u>th</u>ree times a day	
is good at ma<u>th</u>	
<u>th</u>inks it's important to exercise regularly	
<u>th</u>inks it's unheal<u>th</u>y to be <u>th</u>in	
can retell some Greek my<u>ths</u>	
writes <u>th</u>ank you notes when she or he gets bir<u>th</u>day presents	

Review: Language Functions

Giving Advice Video/Audio

Listen to these examples of giving advice. You'll use this function in the next section.

Put It Together

A. What Should I Do? Read the following situations and think of advice for each one.

Situation 1: Michael wants to see the video *Alien*.

Situation 2: Tim is under a lot of stress.

Situation 3: Pam is having trouble sleeping.

Situation 4: Harrison wants to stop smoking.

Situation 5: Brandon has to write a paper about modern art.

Situation 6: Wei wants to get a better score on the TOEFL exam.

Situation 7: Nadia needs information about cultural differences in attitudes towards health.

Your situation: _____

B. Giving Advice. (Pair) Now discuss your advice for each situation with your partner. Do you agree? Follow these directions:

1. Student A gives advice for one of the situations in Exercise A, using the expressions in the boxes on pages 253 and 254. Student A gives degrees of advice, depending on what he or she actually thinks.

2. Student B will agree or disagree with the advice, using the expressions in the boxes in Chapter Seven on pages 224–225, and then give his or her advice. Student B will express degrees of advice and degrees of agreement or disagreement. (See the expressions for degrees of agreement in Chapter Seven, page 226.)

3. Exchange roles.

Part Four Broadcast English: Improving Public Health in Russia

Before Listening

A. Thinking Ahead. (Group)

You are going to listen to a radio program about efforts to improve public health in Russia. The program discusses the issue of **preventive medicine** (or **care**). This is health care designed for people who *are* healthy, in order to *keep* them healthy. Before you listen, discuss the answers to these questions.

1. Do you think it's a good idea to spend money on preventive care? Why or why not?

2. What kinds of preventive health care do you and your classmates practice? Make a list.

B. Predicting. (Pair)

Before you listen, make a prediction about what you are going to hear. Discuss the answer to this question.

• What kind of public health problems do you think exist in Russia today?

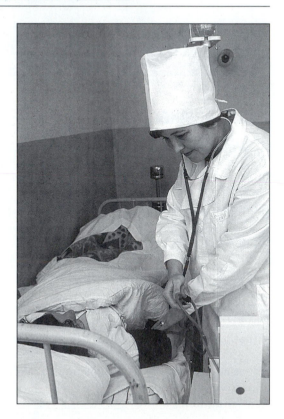

C. Guessing Meaning from Context.   In the radio program, you are going to hear some words that may be new to you. Before you listen, guess the meaning of some of the words from the program. The words are underlined in the sentences. Look for clues to their meaning in the words around them.

Write your guess in the blank after each sentence. Then check your guess with your teacher or the dictionary.

1. Yesterday his health was fine, but today a new problem has <u>emerged</u> and we have to take him back to the hospital.

   Guess: _____

2. He is too <u>feeble</u> to walk—he'll have to get around in a wheelchair.

   Guess: _____

3. My grandmother has lived longer than most of her <u>contemporaries</u>. All of her childhood friends have already died.

   Guess: _____

4. Alcoholism is <u>rampant</u> in Russia. Apparently, it's a serious problem because so many Russians are addicted to alcohol.

   Guess: _____

5. The <u>collapse</u> of Communism in Russia also meant the end of free healthcare.

   Guess: _____

6. I wanted to buy a newspaper, so I asked if there was a newsstand nearby. The man said that there was a <u>kiosk</u> on the next corner.

   Guess: _____

7. You can tell when people are drunk because they can't walk in a straight line. Instead, they <u>stagger</u> down the street.

   Guess: _____

8. They proposed a new law to raise the legal drinking age in that state; the people will vote on the <u>initiative</u> next fall.

   Guess: _____

9. Mothers Against Drunk Drivers is a <u>nonprofit organization</u>. That means it uses any money it receives to pay for the cost of running the organization, such as rent, office supplies, and employees' salaries.

Guess: _____

10. The government is so <u>overburdened</u> by other expenses that it cannot pay for healthcare.

Guess: _____

D. Vocabulary Preparation: Idioms and Phrasal Verbs.   The speakers use some informal expressions and phrasal verbs in the radio program. First, read each sentence and guess the meaning of the underlined word. Then choose their meaning from the definitions in the box. Write the letters in the blanks.

Sentences

_____ 1. Elaine was late for the 9 A.M. meeting, but she finally <u>showed up</u> in the office at around 11 A.M.

_____ 2. Isn't this lamp <u>kitschy</u>? It's a ceramic bear with a fish in its mouth.

_____ 3. I don't want to be the first to <u>cast blame</u>, but it is obvious to me that he caused the project to be late because he comes to work late every day.

_____ 4. The last time I bought a used car I really <u>got shafted</u>: The engine exploded on the way home and the guy who sold it to me wouldn't give me my money back!

_____ 5. You should just tell him <u>straight out</u> that he isn't doing a good job.

Definitions

a. consider someone or something responsible for a bad situation

b. directly

c. was treated unfairly

d. silly, funny, or cheap looking art

e. appeared

Listening

A. Listening for Main Ideas. [Audio] Listen to the radio program. As you listen, try to answer these questions:

- What kind of public health problems are there in Russia?

- How are Russians trying to improve public health?

listening **Strategy**

Guessing Meaning from Synonyms and Paraphrases [Audio]

You can sometimes guess the meaning of a new word by listening for a synonym or a paraphrase of it that you may hear just after the word. Here is an example:

> Preventive healthcare is a better use of our money. Educating people on ways to stay healthy is cheaper than taking care of them after they're already sick.

The speaker has paraphrased "preventive healthcare" in the second sentence. It means "educating people on ways to stay healthy."

B. Guessing Meaning from Context. [Audio] Listen to parts of the program and guess the meaning of the following expressions. Listen for a synonym or a paraphrase to help you guess.

1. cost-effective = _____

   _____

2. personal responsibility = _____

   _____

C. Listening for Details. [Audio] Listen to parts of the program again. Listen for details that answer these questions.

1. Why might public health problems exist in Russia today?

   _____

   _____

2. What are some ways that Russians are trying to solve the alcohol problem?

_____

_____

3. What is the main problem facing those who are trying to improve public health in Russia?

_____

_____

4. What *should* the government of Russia do to help improve public health, according to Serghey Polyatkin?

_____

_____

5. What's cheaper, according to Leonid Malkov, preventive healthcare, or taking care of people who are already ill?

_____

_____

6. What's another benefit of preventive healthcare, according to Leonid Malkov?

_____

_____

After Listening

Discussion. **Group**   Discuss the answers to these questions.

1. What are some health problems in Russia? How are Russians trying to solve these problems?

2. Who is responsible for *your* health?

3. How do you feel about the following? Compare your ideas with your classmates'.

- you have control over your health
- who should pay for healthcare: the government or individuals
- tips for staying healthy
- health treatments

. . : : : : Part Five   Academic English: What Is Good Health?

Before Listening

A. Discussion. Pair   You are going to listen to a lecture about maintaining good health. Before you listen, discuss the answer to this question.

- What is your personal approach to maintaining good health?

B. Predicting. Pair   The lecture contains information about how to develop a personal approach to good health in the following areas. What do you think the speaker will say about each one?

- diet
- weight
- addictive substances
- exercise
- stress
- relationships with others

C. Thinking Ahead.   Look at the outline for the lecture on pages 265–267 and think about your discussion in Exercise A. What would you like to know about maintaining good health? Write two or three questions about the subject.

_____

_____

_____

D. Guessing Meaning from Context.   In the lecture, you are going to hear some words that may be new to you. Before you listen, guess the meaning of some of the words from the program. The words are underlined in the sentences. Look for clues to their meaning in the words around them.

Write your guess in the blank after each sentence. Then check your guess with your teacher or the dictionary.

1. That doctor practices <u>holistic</u> medicine, so she will ask you about your emotional state as well as give you a physical examination.

   Guess: _____

2. Some people believe that the <u>harmony</u> of both mental and physical health is necessary for feeling good.

   Guess: _____

3. Before, Sue was sick all the time. Now she feels great. The <u>adoption</u> of a healthier lifestyle was the key.

   Guess: _____

4. Sue wants to <u>enhance</u> her appearance, so she's going to get a fashionable haircut.

   Guess: _____

5. I know he will be a successful doctor because in medical school he showed a great deal of <u>potential</u> for understanding the causes of and cures for disease.

   Guess: _____

6. Since it's impossible to get money for preventive healthcare at the government level in Russia, ordinary people are working at the <u>grassroots level</u> and raising their own money.

   Guess: _____

7. Some people believe that having a happy, <u>intimate relationship</u>—a successful marriage, for example—is good for your general health.

   Guess: _____

academic Strategy

Reading Questions Before Listening

Whenever you can see them, it's a good idea to read listening comprehension questions before you actually listen to a lecture. This prepares you for listening and makes your listening more focused because you may know *exactly* what to listen for. For example, if you see this question,

> What are three differences between public health issues in Russia and public health issues in the United States?

you know to listen for "three differences" once the lecture starts.

When you read a listening comprehension question before you listen, look for key words that tell you what to listen for. Common key words include numbers, examples, and concepts such as "the most" and "the least," similarities and differences, and causes and results.

Practice. Read the following questions about a passage on Americans' greatest health fears. Underline the words in the questions that tell you what to listen for.

1. What disease do Americans fear the most?

2. What is the difference between what women fear and what men fear?

3. What are some examples that illustrate the fact that Americans are taking more responsibility for their own health than they have in the past?

Listening

A. Listening for the Main Idea. **Audio** Listen to the lecture one time. Don't take notes. Don't worry about understanding everything. Just listen for the main idea. As you listen, try to answer this question:

- What does it mean to be healthy, according to the lecture?

B. Taking Notes: Using an Outline. **Audio** Listen to the lecture again. This time fill in the outline.

What is Good Health?

I. The Meaning of Health

    A. Simple definition of health: _____

_____

B. Holistic definition of health: _____

_____

II. The Concept of Health Promotion

A. Health promotion involves _____

_____

B. Good health requires _____

_____

C. Poverty is _____

D. Health maintenance involves these sectors of society: _____

_____

III. Health Promotion Around the World

A. Global health promotion must be adapted to _____

_____

B. Role of World Health Organization: _____

_____

C. Example of grassroots activity: _____

_____

IV. Developing a Personal Approach to Good Health

A. Diet: _____

_____

B. Exercise: _____

_____

C. Weight: _____

_____

D. Stress: _____

_____

E. Alcohol, drugs, cigarettes: _____

_____

F. Social responsibility: _____

_____

Now listen again and complete the outline.

C. Listening for Details. `Audio`   Listen to parts of the lecture again. Listen for details that answer these questions. Read the questions before you listen.

1. What are five examples of the basic elements that an individual requires for good health?

_____

_____

2. What is the greatest threat to good health worldwide?

_____

_____

3. What is the result when different sectors of a society (such as government, business, healthcare, and schools) all work together?

_____

_____

After Listening

Using Your Notes. **Group**   Use your notes to discuss these questions about the lecture.

1. What does it mean to be healthy? Is there more than one way to define "healthy"?

2. What do the following have to do with maintaining good health?

    • diet

    • exercise

    • weight

    • stress

    • addictive substances

3. Do you disagree with any of the information in the lecture? What do you disagree with? Why?

4. Is anything missing from the lecture? Is there something important for maintaining health that the lecture did not cover?

 Step Beyond

You are going to give a short presentation on a cultural aspect of health. Your presentation will consist of a comparison on how important the following issues are in two cultures or countries. You may want to compare how important the issues are or the attitudes toward the issues in two cultures or countries.

• diet

• exercise

• weight control

• stress

• addictive substances

• social and personal relationships

• your topic: _____

Step One

First, choose a topic that interests you. Then do Web or library research, or find information in an introductory health textbook. You are going to present your ideas from notes (see Chapter Four, page 143), so as you do your research, take notes on index cards or use a form like the following.

Your Topic: _____

Country A: _____	Country B: _____
Examples:	Examples:

Step Two

Go over your notes and organize your information. Decide on a time limit for each presentation. A good length is from three to five minutes.

speaking Strategy

Making Comparisons

There are several words and expressions to use when you make comparisons. Some emphasize similarities. Others emphasize differences. Some do either. Here are a few words and expressions:

Similarities	**Differences**	**Either**
Both . . . and . . .	Although . . .	more than
Neither . . . nor	. . . but . . .	less than
Similarly . . .	However . . .	

Examples:

- Studies show that citizens of <u>both</u> Country X <u>and</u> Country Y tend to be about 15 percent overweight.

- Citizens of Country X feel that alcoholism is the most serious public health issue. <u>However,</u> citizens of Country Y think that poor nutrition is the most serious public health problem that they face.

- Citizens of Country Y are <u>more</u> likely to visit a doctor regularly <u>than</u> are citizens of Country X.

Step Three

Present your information. Follow these guidelines:

✓ paraphrase information from your research

✓ stay within the time limit

✓ use your notes; don't read

✓ make eye contact with your group members

✓ use expressions for making comparisons

✓ take and answer questions from your group members when you are finished

Step Four

Form small groups and evaluate each other's presentations. Use the following questions in your evaluation:

✓ Were the presentations easy to understand?

✓ Were the issues interesting?

✓ Did the speakers use notes and make good eye contact?

✓ Did the speakers support their opinions with good reasons?

✓ Did the speakers make clear comparisons?

Instructions for Information Gap

Chapter Four, Part Two, After Listening

Exercise A, Page 116

Student B

It's a good idea to review Greek myths and legends when you study ancient Greek art. This is because ancient Greek art often **depicts** (shows) subjects from myths and legends. An important part of Greek mythology is the gods and goddesses. People who study art need to know their Greek and Roman names and the characteristics or activities that they represent. How much do you already know about them? (Refer to the vocabulary chart for help with difficult words.)

Ask your partner for the missing information and write the answers on your chart. Take turns asking and answering questions. Ask questions such as the following:

B: What is Aphrodite's Roman name?

A: Venus.

A: What is Aphrodite the goddess of?

B: Love and beauty.

Vocabulary

Terms	Meanings
prophecy	knowledge of future events
crafts	the art of making everyday objects that people use or wear, such as furniture and jewelry
commerce	business activities
the underworld	according to ancient Greeks' beliefs, the place where people went after death
fertility	the ability to have many children or to produce large crops
blacksmith	a person who makes things from metal, such as horseshoes

Major Greek Gods and Goddesses

Greek Names	Roman Names	Main Characteristics/Activities
Aphrodite	_Venus_	Goddess of love and beauty
Apollo	Phoebus Apollo	_____ _____ _____
Ares	_____	God of war
Artemis	_____	Goddess of the moon, hunting, and childbirth
Athena	Minerva	_____ _____
Demeter	Ceres	_____
_____	Bacchus	God of wine and fertility
Eros	_____	God of love
_____	Juno	Goddess of marriage; protector of women
Hephaestus	_____	God of fire and metalworking; the blacksmith of the gods
Hermes	Mercury	_____ _____
Hades	_____	God of the underworld

appendix 1
Common Irregular Verbs

be am-is-are, was-were, been
beat, beat, beaten
become, became, become
begin, began, begun
bend, bent, bent
bet, bet, bet
bleed, bled, bled
blow, blew, blown
break, broke, broken
bring, brought, brought
build, built, built
burst, burst, burst
buy, bought, bought
catch, caught, caught
choose, chose, chosen
come, came, come
cost, cost, cost
creep, crept, crept
cut, cut, cut
dig, dug, dug
dive, dove *or* dived, dived
do, did, done
draw, drew, drawn
drink, drank, drunk
drive, drove, driven
eat, ate, eaten
fall, fell, fallen
feed, fed, fed
feel, felt, felt
fight, fought, fought
find, found, found
fit, fit, fit
flee, fled, fled
fly, flew, flown
forget, forgot, forgotten

freeze, froze, frozen
get, got, got *or* gotten
give, gave, given
go, went, gone
grind, ground, ground
grow, grew, grown
hang, hung, hung
have, had, had
hear, heard, heard
hide, hid, hidden
hit, hit, hit
hold, held, held
hurt, hurt, hurt
keep, kept, kept
know, knew, known
lay, laid, laid
lead, led, led
leave, left, left
lend, lent, lent
let, let, let
lie, lay, lain
lose, lost, lost
make, made, made
mean, meant, meant
meet, met, met
pay, paid, paid
put, put, put
read, read, read
ride, rode, ridden
ring, rang, rung
rise, rose, risen
run, ran, run
say, said, said
see, saw, seen
sell, sold, sold
send, sent, sent

set, set, set
sew, sewed, sewn
shake, shook, shaken
shine, shone, shone
shoot, shot, shot
show, showed, shown
shrink, shrank, shrunk
shut, shut, shut
sing, sang, sung
sink, sank, sunk
sit, sat, sat
sleep, slept, slept
speak, spoke, spoken
spend, spent, spent
split, split, split
spread, spread, spread
stand, stood, stood
steal, stole, stolen
stick, stuck, stuck
strike, struck, struck
swear, swore, sworn
sweep, swept, swept
swim, swam, swum
take, took, taken
teach, taught, taught
tear, tore, torn
tell, told, told
think, thought, thought
throw, threw, thrown
understand, understood, understood
wake, woke *or* waked, waked
wear, wore, worn
win, won, won
wind, wound, wound
write, wrote, written

credits

Photo Credits

Unit Openers ©PhotoDisc, Inc.

Chapter 1 Opener: ©PhotoDisc, Inc.; p. 4 (top, left), p. 4 (middle, left), p. 4 (bottom): ©PhotoDisc, Inc.; p. 4 (top, right): ©Ed Taylor Studio/FPG; p. 4 (middle, right): ©CORBIS/Sandy Felsenthal; p. 8, p. 17, p. 12: ©The McGraw-Hill Companies, Inc.

Chapter 2 Opener: ©PhotoDisc, Inc.; p. 34: Lionel J-M Delevingne/Stock Boston; p. 35: ©PhotoDisc, Inc.; p. 38, p. 41: ©The McGraw-Hill Companies, Inc.; p. 44: ©Amy Ritterbusch/Stock Boston; p. 46: ©The McGraw-Hill Companies, Inc.; p. 47: ©CORBIS/Bob Rowan, Progressive Image; p. 50: ©Jim Harrison/Stock Boston; p. 51, p. 57: ©PhotoDisc, Inc.; p. 56: ©Ronnie Kaufman/Stock Market

Chapter 3 Opener: ©Ed Chappell; p. 72: Michael Cassidy. *Waikiki Surf Festival,* 1996. Seventh Heaven Publishers, Vista, CA; p. 74 (left): Donald Judd, *Untitled.* 1967. Lacquer on galvanized iron. The Museum of Modern Art, New York. Helen Achen Bequest (by exchange) and gift of Joseph Helman. Photograph @ 1999 The Museum of Modern Art, New York. ©Estate of Donald Judd/Licensed by VAGA, New York, NY; p. 74 (right): Chuck Close. *Linda.* 1975–76. Acrylic on canvas, 9x7'. Courtesy Pace Wildenstein, New York; p. 75: Andy Warhol: *100 Campbell Soup Cans,* 1962. Albright-Knox Art Gallery, Buffalo, NY (gift of Seymour H.. Knox, 1963). ©1999 The Andy Warhol Foundation for the Visual Arts/Artists Rights Society, New York; p. 77: ©The McGraw-Hill Companies, Inc.; p. 81 (top): Duane Hanson. *Self-Portrait with Model.* 1979. Courtesy, The Collection of Mrs.. Duane Hanson; p. 79: Frank Stella, *Pergusa,* 1981. ©1999 Frank Stella/Artists Rights Society, New York; p. 80 (top): Jasper Johns, *Three Flags,* 1958. Collection, Whitney Museum of American Art, New York. ©Jasper Johns/Licensed by VAGA, New York, NY; p. 80 (bottom): George Segal, *Blue Girl on Park Bench,* 1980. Collection Jeanette, NY; p. 81 (bottom): ©The McGraw-Hill Companies, Inc.; p.. 89 (top): David Smith, *Becca.* 1965. The Metropolitan Museum of Art, NY (purchase, bequest of Adelaide Milton de Groot, by exchange, 1972). All rights reserved. ©Estate of David Smith/Licensed by VAGA, New York, NY; p. 89 (bottom): Louise Nevelson. *City on a High Mountain.* 1983. Steel painted black. 246 x 276 x 162 in. Storm King Art Center, Mountainville, N.Y. Purchase Fund, 1984.4.. Photo by Jerry L. Thompson. ©2000 Estate of Louise Nevelson/Artists Rights Society, New York; p.. 90: Jeff Koons, *Puppy.* 1992. Live flowers, earth, wood and steel. ©Jeff Koons. Photo by Dieter Schwerdtle; p. 93 (left): CORBIS/Massimo Listri; p. 93 (right): ©Joe Schuyler/Stock Boston; p. 100: Jackson Pollock. *Autumn Rhythm.* The Metropolitan Museum of Art, George A. Heam Fund, 1957. (57.92). All rights reserved/Artists Rights Society; p. 101: Robert Rauschenberg. *Canyon.* 1959. ©Robert Rauschenberg/Licensed by VAGA, New York, NY; p. 102: Robert Rauschenberg. *Skyway.* 1964. Dallas Museum of Art, The Roberta Coke Camp Fund, The 500, Inc., Mr. and Mrs. Mark Shepherd, Jr. and General Acquisitions Fund. ©Robert Rauschenberg/Licensed by VAGA, New York, NY; p. 103: Andy Warhol, *200 Campbell's Soup Cans.* 1962. ©2000 The Andy Warhol Foundation for the Visual Arts/Artists Rights Society, New York/Art Resource; p. 104: Claes Oldenburg. *Clothespin.* 1976. Cor-Ten and stainless steel. 45 ft. x 12 ft. 3 1/4 in. x 4 ft. 6 in. (13.72 x 3.74 x 1.37m). Centre Square Plaza, Fifteenth and Market Streets, Philadelphia. Photo by G. Benson/H. Armstrong Roberts; p. 105: Roy Lichtenstein. *Whaam!* 1963. ©Contemporary Arts Services, NY. Tate Gallery, London, Great Britain/Art Resource

Chapter 4. Opener: Erich Lessing/Art Resource; p. 110, p. 137: *Dipylon Vase,* Greek. 8th C., B.C. The Metropolitan Museum of Art, Rogers Fund, 1914. (14.130.14). All rights reserved; p. 112, p. 130: Louvre, Paris/Service de Documentation Photographique de la Reunion des Musees Nationaux; p. 114, p. 118, p. 123: ©The McGraw-Hill Companies, Inc.; p. 124, p. 136: Scala/Art Resource; p. 134: ©PhotoDisc, Inc.; p. 135: *Kouros.* c. 600 B.C.E. Marble, height 6'4". The Metropolitan Museum of Art, Fletcher Fund, 1932. (32.11.1). All rights reserved; p. 138: *Bell Krater,* View: (Side A) Artemis. Attributed to the Pan Painter. James Fund and by Special Contribution, Courtesy of Museum of Fine Arts, Boston; p. 139: *Diadem:* Dionysos and Ariadne in relief. The Metropolitan Museum of Art, Rogers Fund, 1906. (06.1217.1). All rights reserved; p. 142 (top): Art Resource, NY; p. 142 (bottom): Nimatallah/Art Resource; p. 142 (bottom, right): Vatican Museum, Rome

Chapter 5. Opener: Salvador Dali. *The Persistence of Memory.* 1931. The Museum of Modern Art, New York. ©2000 Artists Rights Society, New York; p. 148: ©Ron Lowery/Stock Market; p. 149: ©John Holcroft/Superstock; p. 152, p. 155, p. 161: ©The McGraw-Hill Companies, Inc.; p. 163: ©Superstock; p. 167: ©Manfred Kage/Peter Arnold; p. 174: ©Science Photo Library/Photo Researchers

Chapter 6. Opener: ©2000 The Munch Museum/The Munch-Ellingsen Group/Artists Rights Society, New York/Erich Lessing/Art Resource; p. 182: ©Andre Rouillard/Superstock; p. 183: ©San Diego Union-Tribune; p. 186, p. 189, p. 193: ©The McGraw-Hill Companies, Inc.; p. 194: ©Superstock

Chapter 7. Opener: ©PhotoDisc, Inc.; p. 216, p. 230: ©The McGraw-Hill Companies, Inc.; p. 232: ©PhotoDisc, Inc.; p. 238: ©Toni Michaels

Chapter 8. Opener: ©PhotoDisc, Inc.; p. 248: ©PhotoDisc, Inc.; p. 252, p. 255, p. 259: ©The McGraw-Hill Companies, Inc.; p. 260: ©Dean Conger/NGS Image Collection; p. 265, p. 268: ©PhotoDisc.

Radio Credits

Chapter 1. "Code of Ethics in Business Conference in Tokyo" (Jocelyn Ford, reporter), July 12, 1996, Marketplace. Used with the permission of Marketplace/USC Radio, University of Southern California, Los Angeles, California. **Chapter 2.** "Welfare Systems in Russia, Canada, and Germany" from "The World" (Marina Bouton, interviewer), July 31, 1996, WGBH, Boston. Used with the permission of WGBH, Boston, Massachusetts. **Chapter 3.** "George Segal" from "All Things Considered" (Daniel Zwerdling, host), February 21, 1998, National Public Radio. **Chapter 4.** "Ancient Greek Statues" from "All Things Considered" (Jacki Lyden, interviewer), December 15, 196, National Public Radio. **Chapter 5.** "New Theory Says Sleep Serves to Restore Brain Energy" from "All Things Considered" (Joe Palca, reporter), January 12, 1996, National Public Radio. **Chapter 6.** Excerpt from "What Is Paranoia?" (Michael Phillips, interviewer), January 15, 1995, Social Thought. Used with the permission of Social Thought, San Francisco, California. **Chapter 7.** Excerpt from "Smoking—The 'Gateway' Drug" (Vicki Quay, reporter), August 23, 1996, National Public Radio. **Chapter 8.** "Health Care in Russia" (Emily Harris, reporter), August 16, 1996, Marketplace. Used with the permission of Marketplace/USC Radio, University of Southern California, Los Angeles, California.

Copyright © 1993, 1994, 1996, 1997, 1998 by National Public Radio. These news reports by various NPR reporters were originally broadcast on National Public Radio's "Morning Edition®," "All Things Considered®," "Talk of the Nation®," "Weekend All Things Considered®," and "Weekend Edition®" and are used with the permission of National Public Radio, Inc. Any unauthorized duplication is strictly prohibited.